HERE AND THERE

Leaving Hasidism, Keeping My Family

Chaya Deitsch

Schocken Books, New York

Copyright © 2015 by Chaya Deitsch

All rights reserved. Published in the United States by Schocken Books, a division of Penguin Random House LLC, New York, and distributed in Canada by Random House of Canada, a division of Penguin Random House Ltd., Toronto.

Schocken Books and colophon are registered trademarks of Penguin Random House LLC.

Library of Congress Cataloging-in-Publication Data
Deitsch, Chaya, author.
Here and there : leaving Hasidism, keeping my family / Chaya Deitsch.
pages cm
ISBN 978-0-8052-4317-8 (hardcover : alk. paper).
ISBN 978-0-8052-4318-5 (eBook).
1. Deitsch, Chaya. 2. Jewish women—Connecticut—New Haven—Biography. 3. Habad. I. Title.
F128.9.J5D45 2015 305.48'8924—dc23 2015010023

www.schocken.com

Jacket images: (top) detail from *The Proposal* by Hendel Lieberman, copyright © Chassidic Art Institute; (bottom) courtesy of the author
Jacket design by Jay Harrison
Book design by M. Kristen Bearse

Printed in the United States of America
First Edition
2 4 6 8 9 7 5 3 1

To my parents, for letting life stay complicated

Contents

HERE AND THERE

Introduction

While I had long intended to write about the family I come from, I always assumed I would chronicle the remarkable stories I'd grown up hearing: about Russia and World War II, about negotiating the displaced-persons system in Europe (where my grandmother accidentally gave her children their first and only taste of Spam), and about building a life in America as devout disciples of the Lubavitcher Rebbe. My role in this narrative, if any, would be minimal. And so I began my research—gathering notes, taping relatives, reading histories, poring over photo albums, even contemplating a "shtetl tour" in Ukraine. We are a long-lived bunch, and I had all four grandparents until my late thirties, not to mention aunts, uncles, and family friends, each of whom had something to say.

One afternoon, I took the train into Brooklyn to interview my great-aunt Anya. She is a natural spinner of tales, her observations spiked with an acid sense of humor. ("If your husband hates your hat, you've done something right!") But even as she happily held court, she puzzled over my hunger for the details of her life and wondered who would want to read about such terrible times. "You will never understand Russia," she said, shaking her finger at me. "You will never understand Stalin. You will never understand the *mentality.* This is a place where a person should not be there."

She was right.

It took several years of writing and rewriting for me finally to acknowledge that something was not working. My attempts to set down my family's history either just lay there limply on the page or panted with clichés about bravery and belief. As Anya had warned, the past was not the place for me. I couldn't bring these tales to life because I had something very different to say. Mine is not a narrative of escape, whether from the shackles of tradition (although I did leave the world in which I'd grown up) or the depredations of the gulag. It is, instead, a memoir of staying connected while moving apart, of traveling simultaneously under and within the radar, of stretching without snapping.

I was fortunate in the family into which I had been born. Coddled by two expansive sets of relatives who had safely planted their feet in the nurturing soil of America, I enjoyed a childhood that was secure and loving, if tightly bound by faith and expectations. I grew up in Connecticut with art classes, piano lessons, home-baked cookies, paper dolls, and trips to Miami Beach, but also with gut-busting Shabbos meals, morning prayers, Chanukah gelt, and wondrous tales of miracle-making rabbis, including, of course, the Lubavitcher Rebbe, Menachem Mendel Schneerson, whose portrait hung in my house and in the house of every Lubavitcher I knew. But there were tensions, too. As a young girl, I chafed at my station, silent and invisible, behind the synagogue curtain and dreaded the prospect of an early marriage and a flock of little ones. As a teenager, I drew no strength from the Rebbe or his teachings, or even from more broadly Jewish practices such as keeping kosher or observing the Sabbath. From early on I was headed in another direction, but I still needed my family. A tribesman to the core, I loved my parents, siblings, grandparents, uncles, aunts, and cousins, although I chose to take a very different life path.

So for me there has never been a sharp break with my family and their world, a distinct "before and after." By now middle-aged, I've been secular for nearly twice as long as I was a practicing Hasid. But my back still gets up when well-meaning friends who are familiar with my background make a point of telling me, with conspiratorial condescension, about the "black hatters" they've spotted at the doctor's or sat next to on a flight to Los Angeles, or the pale, thick-stockinged women they saw shopping for couture at Saks. My first reaction is, Well, why shouldn't they be there? Hasidim have gallbladders, too; they're allowed to lust after fashion. My second is, Why are you telling *me* this? These people have nothing to do with me anymore. I recognize the slippery logic of trying to personally disassociate myself from Hasidism even as I insist that its followers are more or less just like everyone else. But I am unable to divide the world into "them" and "everyone else." On Fifth Avenue, a young Lubavitcher, all dark suit, peach fuzz, and religious zeal, scouts for Jews to whom he can give handmade matzo for Passover. I fasten my eyes on the pavement and scurry past him. Along with my embarrassment, however, I feel protective of this sincere teenager and take offense at snipes, especially from other Jews, directed at these earnest street-corner evangelists. And I smile with relief when someone tells me about a nice conversation she had with "one of those sweet boys."

My world lacks neat categories, although at first glance the boundaries appear stark. Where would I fit my aunt, when we meet for lunch at her favorite café in Crown Heights, world headquarters of Lubavitcher Hasidism, and we both start laughing because, fashion-conscious women that we are, we're both dressed in head-to-toe black? And where would I place my nephew, tzitzis dangling out onto his pants, rolling his eyes as I lecture him about wasting his brain cells on a new video game? Or my mother, the two of us curled up in her bed on Saturday night after Shabbos, watching *Rashomon* on public television? Like the Kurosawa film, the only perspective I can attest to is my own. It's this lens, and no one else's, through which I view my past and bear it deliberately, uneasily, but at the same time gratefully forward.

I

Nisht Ahin und Nisht Aher

Stepping out of the subway, I make my way down Kingston Avenue, the main drag of Crown Heights. The street is bustling on this autumn evening: young couples shop for groceries, teenage yeshiva boys rush to class, gangs of little kids dig into crinkly bags of spicy Bissli, a wildly popular Israeli snack food that falls somewhere between Wheat Thins and Fritos. Most everyone is Lubavitcher, but here and there West Indian men and women are also hurrying, though they will save their errands for their own shops on Nostrand Avenue, three blocks away. Despite the modest skirt and blouse I know to wear, I'm too familiar with the code to fool myself into believing that I'm passing as a member of this community. Little details of my outfit telegraph outsider: the pointy black flats and the retro-nerdy eyeglasses suggest the East Village, or perhaps one of the hipper parts of Brooklyn.

But mostly it's what I'm *not* wearing that gives me away. No wig, no wedding ring, no baby at the hip. I'm obviously pushing forty and bear no visible disabilities that might explain my unmarried state. Neither do I have the earnest, hyperalert look one often sees in newer *ba'alei teshuvah,* newly observant "returnees" who have left behind secular America and landed on what to them might as well be Mars. I fit no pattern; I clearly don't belong here.

A glint of recognition passes across a few faces, distant cousins perhaps or old classmates of my father's; I don't really know for sure. My features are unmistakably Deitsch, but I've been away from the community long enough that all of these bearded, black-hatted men are starting to look alike to me. My peers, girlfriends from summer camp and Catskill bungalow colonies, are nowhere to be seen, no doubt at home making supper for their children. When I reach Montgomery Street and disappear through the courtyard of the corner apartment building, it becomes clear to the locals who I am and why I'm here: Ah, she must be an *ainek'l* of Riva Gurewitz, who was buried yesterday afternoon.

Inside, I try to summon a pang of nostalgia for my grandparents' home, but the disarray quickly overwhelms any sentimentality. The apartment, much smaller and boxier than their old one on Eastern Parkway, has an old curiosity shop feel. Furniture has been shoehorned into every available space—the pink crushed-velvet sofa, the old breakfront that had been converted into a bookcase for my grandfather's *sforim,* a glass-fronted cabinet displaying a jumble of chipped teacups and old photos. On the walls hang portraits of the two most recent Lubavitcher Rebbes: Menachem Mendel Schneerson, who had himself passed away only a few years earlier, and his father-in-law, Yosef Yitzchak Schneersohn, who in the painting is wearing a round fur hat that is more typical of other Hasidic sects than of Lubavitchers. Folded in a corner of one of the side rooms is the hospital bed in which my grandfather, Zaydie Tzemach Gurewitz, had died fifteen months earlier. Once again, all the mirrors in the apartment have been draped with sheets, per the custom during *shivah:* mourners are supposed to be occupied with mourning and not with how they look.

Years earlier, two of my mother's sisters, Aunt Danya who flew in from Argentina and Aunt Miri who flew in from Los Angeles, determined to relieve the apartment of some of its tonnage. Rummaging through the walk-in closet in the front hall, they excavated more than fifty jars of instant coffee and two hundred—two hundred!—cans of tuna fish. My grandmother explained sheepishly that the superette downstairs had had a special: five dollars' worth of free groceries for every twenty dollars purchased. She had chosen items that wouldn't spoil, hidden them from my fastidious grandfather, and then forgotten they were there. She came by her hoarding instinct legitimately, however. Food had been horribly scarce in Russia during World War II, and when the family finally succeeded in escaping, she'd been forced to leave everything behind. If stockpiling tuna and coffee seemed a little crazy amid the abundance of America, in the old country it would have made my grandmother the mayor of Kharkov.

Once I had loved Bubby Riva's clutter. When I was small, my grandparents' apartment seemed like an archaeological site, a modern-day Pompeii yielding amazing new artifacts no matter how many times I dug through its layers. Among its treasures were a Styrofoam ball shellacked with bits of orange and red tissue paper, a black plastic Afro pick with a round handle, a pink sweater shot through with silver thread that my mother forbade me even to try on, lest I be tempted to keep it. One item I particularly fancied was a bald doll who came with an assortment of 1940s hairdos that you affixed with a hat pin. She was womanly, small-breasted in the fashion of that time, with a smooth head, sallow complexion, painted red lips, and one eye that refused to open all the way. I imagined a dark history for her: a tragic love affair, a mother who had died young, a devastating scalp condition. Unlike my Barbies back home, this creature emanated a familiar, vaguely continental *Weltschmerz,* an aura of having seen too much and having to forge ahead nonetheless.

But tonight all I want to do is run away. It's seven o'clock and the stream of visitors is thickening, with several hours to go before hitting critical mass. This is a late-night crowd. I spot my father *davening* with the other men. With no sons to say the thrice-daily kaddish for my grandmother, a son-in-law has agreed to take on the grueling responsibility for the next eleven months. I don't see my mother in the crush, but two of her cousins, Fruma and Shterna, are here. Great-grandmothers by now, they are tall and formidable and, as usual, impeccably turned out: they are never without a brooch on a blazer lapel or a silk scarf carefully tied to hide an unfortunate wattle. *"A mammeh; vass kenn mir zugen?"* they sigh. A mother; what is there to say? Also present is Lazar Brody, a fixture at family weddings—back in the day, he could balance a wine bottle on his forehead while dancing the kazatzke. I'm shocked at how old he's gotten. His beard has gone completely gray and his small, wiry frame is a bit stooped, but his eyes are still bright, his expression open and warm.

I finally find my mother at the back of the room seated on a low chair, one of seven special *shivah* chairs that have been brought in for the grieving Gurewitz sisters. They all look exhausted, but they brighten at my approach. I lean in and suddenly I am five again, kissed and fussed over for no accomplishment other than shared DNA. I have jokingly dubbed the collective a "smother of aunts," but the truth is I cherish these effusions of tribal acknowledgment. While it's obvious to them that I've made different life choices, they don't pry and I have no idea what they imagine my life to be. I offer them only the most superficial details; I don't want to risk losing my connection to them.

At home in New Haven, my mother has been known to climb into bed at eight and fall asleep to old black-and-white movies on TCM. Now, bludgeoned by the chaos in the tiny apartment, she looks as if she's about to cry.

"Poor you," I say to her, sticking out my lower lip in sympathy. "Are you hungry?" Every available surface is covered with large platters of food, but in keeping with *shivah* custom, she is to be served her meals by others.

She shakes her head. "No, but I could use some Advil. I don't know how I'm going to last through another five days of this." I dig through my purse and hand her two pills with a glass of water.

There is a tray of kosher sushi on the table, untouched. I fill a plate for myself and settle into a chair. Everyone is telling stories, not one of which takes place after 1950 or in the United States. They had all left Russia together after World War II, spent time waiting for visas to America in European displaced-persons camps, and then lived near one another in or around New York. They had been spared the Nazi death camps, but not wartime famine or Stalin's gulags.

At Zaydie's *shivah,* one of my aunts had discovered a battered leather portfolio in his private cabinet. It contained a treasure trove of documents: a legal paper trail of the family's journey to America. Assuming the authorities in New York were as duplicitous as the KGB back in Russia, he had locked them away, deciding that they were too precious to throw out but too dangerous to share. One document, from a United States immigration agency, had been issued to my grandfather in 1954. It contained the usual information: Tzemach Gurewitz, born in Kiev in 1907, now stateless, hazel eyes, brown hair, five foot four. On a line labeled "Visible Marks and Peculiarities" someone had typed "none," a bureaucrat's indifference to the black-and-white photo immediately below it, of a man with the haunted expression of a prisoner not ten years out of the gulag.

In a jangle of Yiddish, Russian, and accented English the stories pour forth: identity cards are stolen and recovered, borders are crossed with children hidden in baskets, women travel east toward Uzbekistan, one step ahead of the German army, sitting on trains for weeks at a time while husbands are slaughtered on battlefields or shipped off to frozen work camps. The map of their tribulation is meticulously traced and fiercely debated. Kharkov, Siberia, Samarkand, Lvov, Paris, Havana. Each place signals its own brand of suffering: bombs, typhoid, thieves, border guards, or the bewildering bureaucracy of relief agencies. Occasionally some humor slips in, bitter, a little biting.

I know these stories well but am eager to hear them again. This was existence at its keenest and I am left with the troubling sense that, as unbearable as those times were, to have missed them carries its own burden. My generation, the first born in America, has the luxury of the freedom to choose where and how we wish to live, but with choices come accountability, and with freedom comes guilt.

I'm squeezed in between two of my oldest aunts, Yocheved and Leah. They are both close to seventy, trim and luminously beautiful. They have heard that I am writing about the family and want to share what they remember.

"When we stayed in Samarkand, after Zaydie was taken," Yocheved says, "we lived in a strange little house, a kind of tent. We had no running water, if you can believe it, none. It was my job to go once a day to a place—it was an alleyway, really, behind a building—where you collected water from a drainpipe."

Leah jumps in. "Can you imagine, two little girls standing in line with a bunch of strangers just to get a bucket of water from a pipe in a wall? And then dragging it home without spilling?"

"I don't think you were there," Yocheved says drily. "And it came from the ground, not a pipe. Anyway, I'm older than you so I remember. I was *there*." The soft lilt of her Yiddish-inflected English makes it sound like "dare."

Leah winks at me as if to say, We'll talk later. "It's good to write these stories down," she says. "But Chaya, talk to all of us, so you get it right."

She tilts her head in her sister's direction and I nod, non-committally.

Get it right.

I've spent my entire life trying to negotiate the strands of this narrative. What does it mean to be an American child of European-born Lubavitchers, a family bound together by wartime memories and unswerving belief in a Rebbe? Can I exist outside my history, or did my most defining moments happen before I was born? Is it possible to refuse one's birthright, like begging off a dish you'd rather not eat? Thanks, but I've had my fill of KGB dread and long denim skirts. Unable to escape, however, I float in a middle space, a psychic refugee. *Nisht ahin und nisht aher.* Not here and not there. I've come to tolerate my discomfort. It's like wearing an itchy sweater: if you don't scratch, eventually the tingling disappears, almost. My marks, if less visible now, are no less peculiar than those of my parents and grandparents.

It's been a few months since my grandmother's passing, and I'm in my office, typing away, when I happen to glance at the clock at the bottom of my screen. It's three thirty on a Friday afternoon. I do a quick calculation—mid-December means Sabbath candle lighting is early, a bit past four o'clock—and I call my parents' house. These pre-Shabbos conversations are a ritual with us, a demonstration of my peculiar brand of filial dedication, but I cringe as the phone rings. My father picks up.

"Hi, it's me," I say.

"Hi," he says. "Are you home yet?"

"No, but I'm out the door." My heart sinks with the lie that we both know I've just told him.

"What are you doing for Shabbos?"

Every week, it's the same question, from both of my parents. As if this time I will finally give them the answer that they've never stopped hoping they will hear: That I'm planning to attend services at a nearby shul, where I'll meet the "Stu Schwartz, DDS, of my dreams," as my sisters and I have named him. That a Crock-Pot has materialized on my cramped kitchen counter and is cooking a cholent for tomorrow's lunch. I toy with telling the truth for once: that I'll be at work until six and then plan to meet a friend for a movie, and that on Saturday I'll go to the gym and then shop for shoes. But I don't, of course.

"Oh, nothing really," I say. "Just the usual."

A moment of silence from my father. "Okay, then. Have a good Shabbos."

"You, too. Same to Mom."

When it comes to the particulars of religious observance, my parents and their adult children operate under a strict don't-ask-don't-tell policy. By tacit agreement established back when each of us went off to college, we keep the various aspects of our lives WASPily compartmentalized to avoid the mess of confrontation with our parents. But we're also a tight group, fiercely protective and acutely, if not always accurately, sensitized to one another's moods and silences. To the chagrin of my brothers-in-law, my four sisters and I are in constant communication, relaying news about whom we saw and talked to, and what we're eating, watching, wearing, reading, and worrying about. When Ella broke a tooth skiing, the rest of us knew about it practically before she'd unzipped her parka. My parents are looped into the network for the most part, but with the controversial bits edited out or replaced with religiously acceptable alternatives: Saturday travel is moved to Sunday, new trousers morph into skirts, a steak at Peter Luger's becomes cocktails with work friends, and relationships with inappropriate men simply don't exist. It hurts to think about the wedge these fabrications drive between my parents and me, and the self-diminishment of my life, but difficult truths seem to stick in my gullet. I'm not fooling them, I know, but I can't bear to say difficult things.

Friends have remarked wistfully on my family's closeness. We were not ever thus, I hasten to assure to them. As children, we fought and argued as all siblings do, jostling for emotional and physical territory, for sole parental attention. And being the eldest, I surely grabbed, or at least demanded, more than my fair share. Today, I know how fortunate I am to have the family relationships that I do, but I also know that clannishness has its price:

subsuming the self for the good of the collective. In fact, this type of intense bonding isn't unusual in our circles. As with most Lubavitchers, loyalty and obedience have been hardwired into our brains, spooned into us like pabulum since birth.

The practice of Orthodox Judaism today encompasses a web of variations that may seem like hairsplitting to outsiders but are crucial to its practitioners. At the baseline, Orthodox Jews keep kosher, observe the Sabbath, celebrate the festivals and holidays, and educate their children at some type of Jewish school. Married women immerse themselves in the *mikvah,* or ritual bath, each month, seven days after their periods have ended, so that they may resume sexual relations with their husbands. Men wear yarmulkes or some sort of head covering throughout the day—or at the very least when eating and praying. The men pray three times a day (women have a bit more flexibility with prayer requirements, as befits the sex that, in this world, anyway, is primarily responsible for child care) and before morning prayers they don a *tallis* and *tefillin,* the traditional prayer shawl and phylacteries. But as with any highly regimented community, small deviations have outsized implications. There's kosher and then there's glatt kosher. Even more expensive than regular kosher meat, glatt kosher meat comes from an animal whose lungs contained no adhesions or scarring, which would require further inspection and rabbinical ruling about the animal's kosher status. There are kosher dairy products and then there's *Cholov Yisroel,* that is, dairy products made from milk that has been supervised by observant Jews from the moment it has left the cow. There is the routine inspection and washing of fruit and vegetables to rid them of forbidden insects, and then there are the people who buy industrial-grade light boxes and special soaps in their search-and-destroy efforts. Appearances are also examined microscopically. Men may wear beards of various styles and lengths, and some choose to be clean shaven (electric shaver only). Married women may cover their hair with wigs and/ or scarves or with hats that leave some of their hair visible. Some married women cover their hair only in shul. The size, style, and color of a man's yarmulke, whether a woman wears pants, how short her sleeves are, how long her skirts are—all of these nuances broadcast to those in the know where one fits into the Orthodox Jewish scheme of things. Like the thousands of silk threads that imprisoned Gulliver, we are held fast by minutiae.

Being Hasidic adds additional layers. Hasidim are known not only for their strict interpretation of halachah, or Jewish law, but also by their fidelity to a particular Rebbe, who serves as the community's moral authority and to whom followers appeal for blessings and advice. More controversially, the Rebbe is revered by his adherents as a person on such a high spiritual and religious level that he can serve as their intermediary to God—a role that often makes non-Hasidic Orthodox Jews uncomfortable. Hasidism itself is likewise splintered into many branches, each with its own Rebbe, who usually inherited the mantle from his father or other close relative. Here, too, one is pegged by the cut of one's jib. The style of the frock coat and of the fur-trimmed hat, the brim of the felt hat, the length of the side lock—all of these will differentiate at a glance a Gerer Hasid from a Satmar, a Viznitzer, or a Bobover.

It was a lapsed Bobover who told me that other Hasidim barely consider Lubavitchers Hasidic. The Lubavitch movement is unique in its commitment to reaching out to unobservant and assimilated Jews and in the high-profile and tech-savvy nature of its outreach campaigns. The group derives its name from the Ukrainian town of Lubavitch, where the movement had its beginnings early in the nineteenth century. It also goes by Chabad, an acronym for *chochmah, binah,* and *da'as,* the Hebrew words for "wisdom," "knowledge," and "understanding." The outer trappings of its adherents are more modern as well. The image some may have of Hasidim in general—of women in plain, dark clothing and seamed stockings, of men with long, dangling side locks and round fur hats—doesn't pertain here. The Lubavitcher women I know wear modest but stylish dresses and staggeringly high heels; their human-hair wigs cost several thousand dollars apiece. The men have long, untrimmed beards but often dress in typically American clothing; my father goes to work in baggy khakis and a collared knit shirt, the fringes of his tzitzis discreetly tucked under his clothes. While it's true that over the past few decades the public face of Lubavitch has become increasingly associated with proselytizing and Messianic fervor, there's a substantial faction who are quietly lenient in their views. In the Lubavitch world that I know, some people own televisions and go to movies or watch them on DVDs; most surf the Internet. They travel widely, read secular literature, and subscribe to *The Wall Street Journal* and *National Geographic.*

Growing up in New Haven, far away from the prying eyes of the Lubavitcher epicenter in Crown Heights, my sisters and I were indulged a little more than most. When we were young, my parents allowed us to eat *Cholov Akum*—that is, kosher but non–*Cholov Yisroel* milk and cottage cheese from the supermarket, as well as Hershey's Kisses and Carvel ice cream cones, which we got almost every Sunday. I wore pants and short sleeves right up to my bas mitzvah and went to school with boys until high school, although casual dating was out of the question. We didn't hide our television in an upstairs closet, as some of my Brooklyn friends did, and I watched everything from *Captain Kangaroo* to *Valley of the Dolls*. My reading was never censored.

My family has deep roots in Lubavitch, on both sides. Unlike the thousands of newcomers, we are what is known as *gezhe,* Hasidim who came from the old country and can trace their ancestry almost to the beginning of the movement at the dawn of the nineteenth century.

Among Lubavitchers today, devotion to the late Menachem Mendel Schneerson, the most recent and, most likely, last Rebbe, is complete and unquestioned, as is the faith in his superior wisdom. As a girl in Crown Heights, my mother remembers the thrill of the Rebbe greeting her by name when she stood in line for his blessing; when her family lived in Cuba, after the war, my zaydie and the Rebbe maintained a regular correspondence. My paternal grandfather consulted the Rebbe before making major business decisions. The Rebbe had encouraged him to open a plastics factory in New Haven, foretelling financial success if he raised enough funds to open a boys' yeshiva in Crown Heights. It still feels strange for me to pass the Oholei Torah school on Eastern Parkway and see the brick building dedicated in big black letters to Mendel and Hinda Deitsch, my great-grandparents.

As a child, I was afraid of the Rebbe, believing he could read my dark and secret thoughts. And the sustenance my parents drew from his guidance could not nourish me. To me, he was an obstacle, a spoiler who put the kibosh on fun and threw up a wall between my non-Hasidic friends and me. Lying in bed at night, I fantasized about waking up the next morning a "regular" Jew, unencumbered by this strict, distant paterfamilias.

My parents, born in wartime, found stability in tradition, reassurance in the infallibility of the Torah. Like most parents, they assumed I would crave the same life: marry young to someone whose pedigree they knew, create a welcoming, kosher home for my husband and children, and find unobtrusive outlets in books and the arts. That wasn't enough for me. It would have been easier in some ways to take the path of least resistance, but time and again I found myself tempted by an unfamiliar glimmer in the distance, a new exit ramp that might bring me to a different destination. I went for it, but all the while I carefully laid a trail of bread crumbs behind me.

2

Upstairs with the Ladies

I was born in Brooklyn on the last Friday in June 1963, the seventh of Tammuz by the Jewish calendar. Crown Heights and the rest of Brooklyn had been wilting under a weeklong heat wave. That afternoon my father had installed a brand-new air conditioner in their Empire Boulevard apartment. "It was the *very first one* we ever owned," he reminds me each time he recounts the event. "A General Electric." Shortly after Sabbath candle lighting, it was "time to have you," and so my parents—he, twenty-four, and she, almost nineteen—walked around the corner to Lefferts General Hospital, cheered on by neighbors sitting on their stoops to cool off. I arrived at ten that night. Before they'd left the apartment, my father had alerted his friend Bamberger, a barrel-chested, red-bearded giant, to meet him at the hospital. As soon as I appeared, Bamberger ran back to tell the local relatives the good news, and then returned to the hospital to walk my father home in the wee hours of Shabbos morning. When my father finally sank into bed, the air-conditioning had been running full blast for more than twelve hours. He can still recall the rapture of the chilled air—*his* chilled air—on his sticky skin. "It was a real *m'chayah*," he says, a distracted half smile on his face. *M'chayah*, something that is life-enhancing. He does not remark on the connection between his blissful reaction and my name, Chaya, which also means "life," and although as a child I would wait for some sort of big, dramatic finish—something on the order of "but not half as wonderful as you, Chaya"—I knew he was done. Fatherly sweetness isn't his style. My mother, more attuned to her daughter's feelings of self-worth than my father, would add, "They gave me something called Twilight, I fell into a well, and when I woke up they handed me a beautiful baby." It was a little strange, but hearing it always made me happy.

We remained in Crown Heights for a few more months while my father completed his rabbinical studies at the Lubavitcher *kollel*, a common practice among newly married men of scholarly bent. Some eventually went on to become practicing rabbis, and others simply used their time there to acquire another layer of Talmudic armor before they left the yeshiva world to earn a living. Then the three of us left the City on the Hill for the Diaspora of New Haven, where, as Rabbi Deitsch (nonpracticing), my father joined his family's plastics business. It wasn't easy for my mother, just barely out of her teens, to leave her parents and sisters behind. She had never lived away from home, not even for summer camp, but she rallied with visions of a house with a backyard and her own car (once she got a driver's license). She was also now able to put more than eighty miles between herself and the neighborhood yentas, as she and my father settled down to begin their new life together. My parents met through my mother's sister Yocheved and her husband, who knew my father as a yeshiva student. Their respective family backgrounds had made them both excellent "catches," but they were also like-minded, smart, and kind, and, over the course of the few months that they dated, they fell in love.

Family legend has it that my father, a man who has the ability to communicate a considerable amount of information by actually saying very little, proposed on the subway by turning to my mother and saying *"Nu?"* This Yiddish exclamation could mean anything from "So, why does it take you so long to get ready to go anywhere?" to "So, do you want to get married?" My mother, shy and movie-star beautiful, evidently understood and replied in the affirmative.

Our first home was the middle-floor apartment of a three-story house situated about halfway between the home of my Deitsch grandparents and the Orchard Street Shul in New Haven's old Jewish neighborhood downtown. Until I was old enough to go to school, I kept myself busy patrolling the block on my red tricycle, playing in the sandbox at Edgewood Park, or tending to my growing collection of dolls. Sometimes my mother and I would visit our upstairs neighbor Pat, whose husband worked long hours at a nearby hospital. More than once, I climbed the stairs alone to get a cookie, freshly baked in Pat's nonkosher oven. The nub of guilt attached to this memory tells me that I was old enough to know better, perhaps two and a half or three. But even then, the lure of a treat was stronger than my fear of punishment. Cookies, in fact, were one of the few things I ate willingly. The long list of food I wouldn't touch included most vegetables, especially tomatoes, all meat and fish, even the cheesecake my parents sometimes brought back from Brooklyn. As a consequence, I was quite underweight, and relatives, remarking on the ridges across my chest, accused my mortified mother of not feeding me. When she discovered me shoveling fistfuls of sand into my mouth at the playground, she placed a panicked call to our pediatrician, Dr. Lattanzi, who told her not to worry, that I was just looking for minerals. Thus began daily administrations of Carnation Instant Breakfast, whose chalky thickness no chocolate or strawberry flavor could mask. Wanting to get the torture over with as quickly as possible, I would slurp it up through a big plastic straw, trying not to gag. Seeing the empty glass, my mother's face would brighten.

"See, you do like it!" she'd exclaim. "Have another one." That rarely worked.

If I wasn't an eater, I was certainly a talker, gabbing away in full sentences by age one. *"Voss is doss?"* What's this? I'd ask, pointing a small finger at some object. *"Kleidele,"* I'd say as my mother slipped a dress over my head, and *"shichelach,"* as I lifted a leg bearing a patent-leather Mary Jane. My parents, who spoke English to each other and to their contemporaries, slipped naturally into Yiddish when they spoke to babies and anyone over sixty. But I soon abandoned my mother tongue, preferring the English of the storybooks my mom picked up at the public library and the children's songs she played on the little turntable that magically turned back into a suitcase when we weren't using it. English had another advantage in that it made eavesdropping that much more effective. A compulsive watcher of people, I hungrily took in conversations, clothing, facial expressions, body types, and small scenes of human interaction. These details I harvested for later use in daydreams and fantasies. Two big kids at the park, one with a long braid, each trying to go higher than the other on the swings. A woman wearing shiny black boots that went up past her knees. My teenage aunt and her school friends sprawled across her bed, laughing and shouting. With eyes the size of yo-yos, I would gape, unblinking, until the objects of my curiosity caught me looking or moved out of range. My mother tried to break me of the habit.

"Stop staring," she whispered. "It's not polite." We were in the waiting room at Dr. Lattanzi's office, and I was transfixed by a woman and the little boy crying by her side. My mother tried to distract me with a book but I ignored her until she grabbed me and turned me so that I was facing her. "But they're so interesting," I protested. He was leaning into his mother's lap, and she was stroking his hair. I wondered what had made him cry and whether he'd feel better if he played with one of the toys scattered around the waiting room. There was a child-size table in the corner, with switches that let you light up colored shapes on the surface, a particular favorite of mine.

"It makes people uncomfortable," she said firmly. I tried to obey but, like an addict, kept sneaking looks at the pair until I was nabbed again.

At some point it occurred to me that if I kept my eyes on the objects of my interest but turned my head in a different direction, they might not realize they were being watched. I conducted a trial at my grandparents' house one day as my father and uncle stood and talked nearby. Positioning myself to their right, I stared straight ahead and slowly rotated my eyeballs left. I suddenly felt a sharp pain at the back of my scalp as Uncle Beryl yanked on my hair.

"Hey kid, what're you doing with your head?"

I said nothing and slunk away, my face hot with shame. But my fascination with the world outside my own small part of it never went away.

I saw my father's parents—Bubby and Zaydie Deitsch—nearly every day. Their house, a large green Victorian across the street from the park, presented endless possibilities for an indulged eldest granddaughter, provided nothing got broken. In nice weather, I spent much of my time on the porch, a wraparound surrounded by a stand of small evergreens. Climbing over the back railing and easing myself onto the ground, I'd find myself in a magical forest, dark, cool, and smelling faintly of the dog poop deposited by the neighbor's Labrador. Inside the house, I wandered undisturbed through the warren of spotlessly kept rooms, poking through cabinets, drawers, boxes, and closets, occasionally retrieving a tchotchke—a hair ribbon, a pen—that I might be allowed to take home. Atop the out-of-tune piano in the small parlor off the living room rested a delicate porcelain figurine, an old-fashioned horse and carriage with a young woman's lovely blond head peering out discreetly from behind a curtain. I coveted it with all my heart but was too afraid to touch it, let alone ask if I could have it. Instead I studied it from a respectful distance, trying to imagine what the inside of the carriage looked like and where the lady was going in such haste. Catty-corner to the piano was "Zaydie's desk," although I never once saw him sit at it. One of the side drawers was filled three-quarters of the way up with pennies and the occasional nickel or dime—detritus from my grandfather's trouser pockets. Plunging my hands deep into the pile of cold metal, I would wriggle my fingers to feel the coins slither over my skin. Then I'd grab two handfuls and dump them onto the carpet to arrange them into various shapes, always slipping the brightest penny into my mouth to savor the shivery metallic tang on my tongue.

I usually played alone in my grandparents' house. There were no cousins my age living in New Haven, and my sister Ricki, born when I was three months shy of my second birthday, was too little to be of any interest to me. The constant buzz of adult activity—my father's youngest sister, a high school senior who still lived at home; assorted aunts and uncles rotating through with new babies in tow, all bound together by the family business and the force field of Bubby's kitchen—was not hard to tune out. By late afternoon, my grandmother, house kerchief neatly wound around her head, full-size apron protecting her prodigious bosom, would be pulling pan after pan of broiled meat and chicken from the oven, while a kugel of some kind rested on the counter. If it was past six p.m. on a weekday, my grandfather would be seated at the head of the small kitchen table, digging into a rib steak, a shot glass of Canadian Club within reach. *"L'chaim, l'chaim,"* he would mutter to no one in particular as he drained the glass and wiped his mouth on the back of his hand. His after-dinner kisses left a smear of grease on my cheek and the sweet, shuddering smell of whiskey in my hair.

I would enter the kitchen only under direct orders from my grandmother. "Chaytze, come have chicken!" she would call, her voice cracking slightly from the effort. If it had been my mother, I would have ignored the summons until it had blossomed into full-blown yelling and then stomped to the table in a huff. One did not argue with my grandmother, however. The phrase "I'm not hungry" elicited nothing more than a puzzled, slightly annoyed look. Without knowing quite how it had happened, I'd find myself sitting in the kitchen before a mountain of flesh, steaming hot and precision-cubed, with promises of a piece of cake or some rugelach if I ate half of it.

In the rare moments that I caught Bubby sitting, I would crawl into her lap and present her with my palm. Taking my hand, she'd sing my favorite Russian nursery rhyme, about a mother crow who boiled a pot of kasha and shared it with everyone but the baby crow. I didn't understand a thing she was saying, but I'd watch her closely as she recited the strange words that accompanied the ritual that she played out on my arm, my body tensing for the big surprise at the end.

Soroka khozyaika, kasha varila (tracing circles in my palm)
Etomu dela, etomu dela, etomu dela, etomu dela (pulling one
   little finger at a time)
A etomu (pause, meaningful look) *nye dela, tseep, tseep, tseep!*
   (tickling my arm all the way up to my shoulder).

I would make her do it again and again, until, exasperated, she would say, "No more," and slide me to the floor.

No matter. I was a child who knew that she was loved.

The summer of my third birthday we moved into a one-family house in the Beaver Hill neighborhood, about a mile away from my grandparents. Lined with neat Tudors and Colonials, it was populated by upwardly mobile Italian, Irish, and Jewish families; we were the first Lubavitcher settlers. Our house, on Colony Road, felt enormous. It had a large backyard, a sunroom where we kept our new television, three bedrooms, a paneled basement, and an unfinished attic that gave you splinters if you walked in it barefoot. Ricki and I shared a room, which my mother decorated with furniture she had picked up at the local flea market and repainted. I claimed my half near the door, to make sure I'd have enough light when I woke up at night, afraid of robbers. It suited me just fine.

That September I also began nursery school at the New Haven Hebrew Day School, embarking on what would be an anxious, complicated love affair with formal education. Every morning at eleven thirty I would wait in our front hallway, shouting for my mother when the school bus pulled up. Colin, the driver, would open the door with his hand lever and call out, "Hello, Sleepy!" which was a nickname I'd earned from my daily practice of conking out on the ride home. Most times I went off happily. I was a child who loved structure. It pleased me to know that before I left school at three thirty there would be arts and crafts, cleanup, story time, snack, and nap; that I had a special hook for my jacket; that Mrs. Lewis would hover over us in a matronly dress, pearls, and thick support hose. I wasn't an especially obedient child—when Mrs. Lewis asked if I had an American name, I told her it was Wilma—but rules made me feel safe, laying boundaries that told me how far I could go before I got into real trouble.

Our school was one of the few remaining relics of a neighborhood that had once resembled a miniature version of New York's Lower East Side, with Jewish bookstores, delis, bakeries, butcher shops, and custom tailors. Housed in a squat brick structure that had been built circa 1910, it was the only yeshiva in New Haven and one of the first Lubavitcher day schools in the country. It had been founded in 1944 by the previous Lubavitcher Rebbe, Yosef Yitzchak Schneersohn. Arriving in New York from Europe in 1940, he'd been shocked by how assimilated into American society Jews had become and by their ignorance of their Jewish heritage. So he sent his emissaries to establish yeshivas in cities throughout the United States that had large secular Jewish communities. Unlike the schools in Crown Heights—which catered to a strictly

Orthodox population, and as a result placed less emphasis on secular studies and maintained a strict firewall between boys and girls—New Haven Hebrew Day School used a lighter touch to make its Judaism palatable to a more worldly and less observant student body, and to their parents as well. Our classes were a mix of Lubavitcher, Modern Orthodox, Conservative, Reform, and unaffiliated kids and were coed through the eighth grade. There were two other Lubavitchers in my class: Tzip, a second cousin on my mother's side, and Shoshana, who would move to Israel with her family before first grade. In the beginning, at least, I felt no different from anyone else.

Only a few snapshots of memory remain from my kindergarten year: The thrill of learning that if you put different letters in front of "at," it made whole new words, like cat, mat, and fat. My first Barbie, the original citizen of what would blossom into a metropolis of tippy-toed, torpedo-breasted mannequins and their lavish accoutrements. The too-long ash that broke off the tip of my teacher's cigarette, leaving a sooty smear on what I believed was my finest artwork ever—an apple tree made of glitter.

My mother is both there and not there. Here she is sitting with me at the kitchen table, teaching me how to read. And there she is standing at the front of my kindergarten classroom, which she visits once a week to teach us the Hebrew and Jewish songs that are beyond the scope of our regular, secular teacher: *Modeh Ani,* to be sung every morning after we wash our hands; songs about loving your friends and putting a penny in the *pushka,* the charity box; a ditty about a *shafan katan,* a little bunny who left the door open and caught a cold.

What I'm missing are her pregnancies: the baby boy who died a few days after he was born, and the child she miscarried five months later. I recall sleeping over at my grandparents' house a lot—Zaydie and I would watch Walter Cronkite together, eating our chicken off TV trays—but I can't remember or even imagine my parents' grief at the loss of those babies. It never really left them, and may have had something to do with how they chose to deal with the challenges my sisters and I sent their way as we grew up.

I was deeply attached to both of my parents, but with my father working long hours at the plastics factory, the only time the two of us spent together was Shabbos mornings, when he and I would make the mile-and-a-half trek to the Orchard Street Shul. Buttoned and bowed in my Shabbos finery, I would try to keep up with him by gripping as much of his hand as I could, my black Mary Janes a blur on the sidewalk. The shul, which had been built in the 1920s, had at one time accommodated three hundred congregants on the High Holidays. But by the mid-sixties membership had shrunk to about half a dozen Lubavitcher fathers and their children, and a loyal cluster of old men who lavished on us chewing gum and Estee's diabetic candies. The building was architecturally ornate, with broad limestone steps and a giant stained-glass Star of David over the front door. Inside the main sanctuary, rows of wooden columns led the eye directly to the room's showpiece— the *aron kodesh,* the elaborately carved Torah ark that soared into the women's gallery high above the men's section.

Upstairs was where I headed on most Shabbosim, to meet up with Tzip. Elderly Rebbetzin Gordon, the only other occupant of the women's section, would nod a somber greeting and go back to her prayer book. We'd begun learning Hebrew in first grade, starting with the morning prayers in the siddur. "Enunciate carefully," our teacher had warned us. "Each word creates an angel, but if you pronounce it incorrectly the angel comes out crippled." I took her caution to heart, imagining hordes of limping beings with broken wings and half faces wondering what they'd done to deserve being created this way. But Tzip and I didn't bother much with *davening* in shul. This was our playground, and we preferred entertaining ourselves with a game we'd invented, racing up and down the rows of empty seats, propping up the stands that were supposed to hold the prayer books and then releasing them one by one with a crash, until a sharp *"Girls!"* from Rebbetzin Gordon sent us to the basement to watch the *gabbai* prepare for the kiddush that immediately followed services. As he set out the platters of pickled herring, Manischewitz Tam Tams crackers, marble cake, and bottles of schnapps and Cott orange soda, we clutched our bellies, moaning about starvation, but he invariably shooed us away.

The one participatory act Tzip and I performed during the service came right before the Torah reading. When we heard the jingle of the silver ornaments that had been placed on the Torah scroll, we ran into the men's section, where Rabbi Bernstein would carry the Torah up and down the aisles before bringing it to the *bimah*, the large table on which it would be laid out and unrolled. As he passed by the men, each one would kiss the tip of a finger that had been covered by his tallis and then reverentially place the covered finger on the worn velvet Torah cover. When he came to where we were standing, Tzip and I would each carefully plant a kiss on the Torah cover, too, as the old men smiled down at us. Then we'd go back to our games.

If it was a holiday—Sukkos, Pesach, or Shavuos—I would make

another brief appearance in the men's section, about two-thirds of the way through the *davening*. My father would look up to the balcony and motion for me to come downstairs and stand next to him for *birchas kohanim,* the priestly blessing. It dates back to the blessing that the first *kohen,* Moses's brother, Aaron, bestowed upon the Children of Israel in the Sinai Desert. Today, the ritual is performed by his male descendants during the holiday service. Because it's believed that God is particularly present at this time, the congregation is not supposed to look as the *kohanim* stretch out their hands and chant the prayer. My father would pull his tallis all the way over his head and over mine, and we'd listen as the hazan, the prayer leader, led the blessing's call and response, the *kohanim* slowly and deliberately echoing his words one at a time. My father would point to each word in the siddur as it was chanted, tapping on the page at the blessing's end, when it was time for the congregation to reply with a loud and vigorous *"Ahmeyn!"* If I behaved nicely, my father would twist one of the fringes at the ends of his tallis into a point and tickle my ear with it. Cocooned in his tent, I breathed in the warmth of his fingers, the gamey wool of his prayer shawl, the varnish of the bench. I felt secure and special.

The long walk back home from shul was always a trial, since nothing, not even weary children, could be carried in the street on Shabbos. In an effort to keep me moving, my father and grandfather would cheat a little, each grabbing one of my hands and swinging me between them in the air. "One, two, three, *wheee!*" they'd say as they took a giant step forward, and I'd laugh as I became weightless in their grip. They repeated the game all the way to my grandparents' house, where we'd drop off Zaydie and then trudge the rest of the way home, with no swinging at all.

One Shabbos the three of us encountered an elderly woman walking toward us accompanied by a little white dog. I stiffened; there were very few animals I wasn't terrified of. As we came closer, the woman said something to the dog in Russian. My grandfather's expression suddenly changed into one of rage. Looking fiercer than I'd ever seen him, he barked something at her in Russian, and she scurried away. The woman had commanded the tiny dog to "bite the Jews," my father explained later, and my grandfather had growled, "If it does, I'll break its neck." *Slamayu sheyu.* My heart flooded with pride and wonder. I knew that Zaydie's anger had something to do with "the war" that the adults often talked about.

This sense of connection to the men in my family vanished as I approached my preteen years. Shul no longer felt as welcoming. No one told me not to come downstairs anymore, but in my frilly Shabbos dress and fancy kneesocks, even I realized that I no longer belonged among the dark-suited men and boys. I felt like an upstart crashing a party of elites, and I scurried back to my proper sphere upstairs, losing my cherished connection to my father along the way. I would spend the rest of my childhood trying to adapt to my new circumstances, but it felt like a pale imitation of the real thing. Stuck behind the curtain, whispering the prayers to keep my woman's voice from being heard by the men, I had turned into a moon drawing light from a distant star. It was not a good feeling.

3

A Wedding in Crown Heights

One Sunday in early September, two months after I'd turned seven, my mother herded Ricki and me into the car and then eased herself into the passenger side in the front, huffing a little from the effort. She was eight months pregnant, and her belly was now the size of a watermelon. We were headed to Crown Heights for the wedding of Aunt Miri, my mother's youngest sister, which would take place the following Sunday, and we'd be camping out in Zaydie and Bubby Gurewitz's apartment for the week. My father would drive back to New Haven later in the day and rejoin us on Friday afternoon.

My mother's physical discomfort made her even more snappish than she usually was before trips to Crown Heights. She and my father had been arguing over luggage—she was a horrible overpacker—and now he sat sullenly behind the wheel. Ricki and I knew to keep our mouths shut.

I sat back and stationed myself purposefully at my window. I'd invented a game of silently marking our time with the changing terrain. By now we'd traveled to Crown Heights so often that I could clock the two-hour drive almost to the minute. As we'd done a hundred times before, we eased onto Merritt Parkway, going less than a mile before my father pulled the car onto a grassy shoulder and reached for the dog-eared miniature siddur that he kept in the glove compartment. Opening it to the bookmarked page, he recited the Traveler's Prayer aloud in Hebrew. I waited for my favorite part, which I'd read in the English translation.

> *V'satzilainu mikaf kol o'yaiv v'oraiv, v'listim v'chayos ra'os ba'derech.* . . .
> And deliver us from every enemy and ambush, and from robbers and wild beasts on the journey. . . .

I imagined horse-drawn carts on the Merritt, steered by nervous Hasidim in fur-and-velvet frock coats on the lookout for lions and malevolent leather-booted gangs. Hiding behind a stand of elms, they would pounce, only to be restrained by some miraculous divine force. My father completed the prayer, and after we emphatically answered *"Ahmeyn!"* he nosed the car back onto the highway.

A few minutes later I held my breath while we wobbled over the slippery metal grid of the Sikorsky Bridge and then settled into mile after mile of dense foliage, catching glimpses of expensive ranch houses in Fairfield County—a placid part of Connecticut that had little to do with New Haven's urban thrum. We passed the sign for Norwalk, and my mother fiddled with the AM radio dial until she found WEVD, which proudly proclaimed itself "the station that speaks your language." She and my father shook their heads and laughed at the corny prattle of Art Raymond, an old-fashioned tummler who played Yiddish songs and told stories. My Yiddish was no longer up to the task—it was stuck at the level of a three-year-old—and so I simply tuned out, relieved that my father wasn't making us listen to a football game and that the tension in the car had finally broken.

We entered New York State via the hairpin turns of the Hutchinson River Parkway and crossed the steely grandeur of the Whitestone Bridge. In Queens, I flinched repeatedly as one car after another seemed to veer within inches of us, only to swerve back into its own lane seconds before impact. I wondered at the travelers roaring past—hot-rodders in bright red Corvettes, multiple generations of Indians packed into late-model sedans, limo drivers headed to JFK airport, other Hasidic families like ours.

"Look, girls! It's the globe from the World's Fair," my mother said, pointing, as she did on every trip, to the giant Unisphere. "Daddy and I went there when you were a baby, Chaya." I read the sign for Flushing Meadows and giggled at the thought of a meadow filled with toilets.

My father drove steadily on, seemingly unfazed by our constant brushes with death. Finally, the last exit of the Interboro Parkway brought us into East New York. We turned left onto Eastern Parkway and passed my father's old yeshiva (now a Baptist church) and a string of chop shops with rows of hubcaps glinting like mirrors along chain-link fences. I stared at the African American street life: the well-dressed middle-aged couple clutching Bibles; two women talking on a stoop, wearing identical helmets of pink curlers. On the sidewalk below them, a group of girls my age were playing double Dutch, their legs a blur of brown knees and brightly colored Keds. A man in his twenties with a large blue hair pick firmly anchored in his Afro glanced at our Buick with its out-of-state license plate as we waited for the light to turn green. "Lock your doors," my mother instructed. It was 1970, and the riots of the 1960s had erected walls of mistrust between blacks and whites throughout the country. The Black Panther trial in New Haven in the summer of 1970 had left its own angry mark on our city.

At Schenectady Avenue we began to see Lubavitcher faces, young women pushing strollers weighed down with toddlers and shopping bags, bearded men in dark suits, streams of children coming home from school. In contrast to the unhurried pace of the scene we'd just passed, Sunday was a regular workday for many Crown Heights Lubavitchers, and everyone seemed to be rushing somewhere. It was hard to make out individual faces through the car window, but I knew that would change once we were out on the street. Most of my relatives lived in Crown Heights: my mother's parents and four of her sisters, my father's brother and a sister, plus assorted spouses and an ever-expanding roster of children. Outer circles of kin, second cousins and beyond, were simply too numerous to count. On our walks down Kingston Avenue my parents would inevitably run into someone they knew—a distant relation, an old classmate, a friend from the bungalow colony, or some combination of the three.

"Chaya, do you know who this is?" my mother would say excitedly. "It's my cousin Shmulik, Uncle Hirschel's son." I'd respond with a polite smile, too distracted by the activity on the street to match my mother's enthusiasm. Everyone we passed seemed vaguely familiar, as if perhaps I'd dreamed about them.

My parents seemed to enjoy these encounters, but I had to steel myself each time. The locals, lacking the New England Yankee reserve that I'd grown accustomed to, stared at us with unnerving frankness. I watched them sizing me up and became conscious of my own strangeness refracted through their gaze. Small details betrayed us: our slightly bewildered expressions as we negotiated the crowded sidewalk; our plain skirts and tops, which were not carried in local shops; the way we obediently stopped at the curb and looked for oncoming cars before we crossed the street. While I didn't like standing out, I had no desire to fit in. The lives of people here seemed too crowded.

In truth, my mother was less pleased with these trips than she let on. Preparations for sojourns in Crown Heights were laced with anxiety that built up in our house like a gas, odorless and deadly, leading without fail to arguments, tears, and angry silences. Given New Haven's casual style, at least by Brooklyn standards, my mother worried about us riding into town looking as if we'd just arrived from Dogpatch. And so before each trip she applied herself to the task of family gussying-up like a harried wardrobe mistress just before curtain time. We usually spent Rosh Hashanah, Simchas Torah, and the closing days of Passover in Brooklyn, and in the weeks leading up to our departure, time had to be allocated for expeditions to Rudy's Salon for fresh haircuts and Malley's Department Store for holiday dresses with itchy, stiff crinolines and patent-leather shoes. My father was mostly exempt from my mother's scrutiny. All he needed was a clean yarmulke, a well-brushed fedora, and a dark suit; his sole concession to fashion was a dapper, colorful tie. He was, in any case, impervious to high style. His favorite pair of New Haven pants, a baggy polyester knit with brown and blue checks, cost twelve dollars at Caldor.

My mother agonized longest and hardest over her own ensemble. One afternoon I walked into my parents' bedroom to find her scowling in front of her dresser mirror. She looked pretty, I thought, in a satin top, tailored wool skirt, and my favorite brooch, a large green stone surrounded by pearls and gold filigree.

"Does this look too wiggy?" she asked, picking at the front

curls of her *sheitel* with the pointed tip of a rat-tail comb. I shook my head no, even though I thought that all of her wigs looked pretty fake. With her high cheekbones and full lips, my mother had an excellent face for the kerchiefs and small hats that she usually wore in New Haven. But the big-hair, poufy creations that looked almost natural on other women seemed not to sit quite right on her head, two opposing forces straining to connect.

"You shouldn't worry so much," I said. "Everyone knows it's a *sheitel*." If the hairline looked too real, in fact, people would talk.

She sighed, ignoring me. "I just wish I could dress comfortably."

My grandparents' apartment building on Eastern Parkway was a relic of a more prosperous era, when doctors and other professionals had staked their claim to the neighborhood. It reminded me of a castle: the crenellated brickwork, the long awning leading to the wrought-iron front door, and the rows of small brass buttons with little name tags alongside them. I found GUREWITZ, pressed, and waited for the faint buzz. We crossed the marble lobby and got into the elevator, exiting on the second floor. I always made a point of noting the unmarked door that led to the incinerator, at the bottom of which I imagined an inferno vaporizing smelly trash into nothingness. Apartment living, I decided, was far superior to my plain single-family-home existence, with its boring carpeted staircases and curbside pickup. My seven-year-old eyes didn't register the toll that time and a lack of money had exacted. The marble floors were faded and worn, and safety was an issue even inside the building. My mother had been mugged in the hallway the year before, punched in the face by a man who grabbed her pocketbook and ran.

But none of that mattered now. Stepping out of the elevator, we heard the familiar scrape of the dead bolt and the metallic clunk of the Magic Eye lock being released. The reassuring scent of camphor wafted toward us as my grandfather opened the door first a crack, then all the way. My mother broke into a wide smile and ran toward him; whatever tension she had been feeling vanished at the sight of her father. It was beyond my understanding that a grown-up could be homesick. Not until much later in life did I try to piece together the narrative of her years as a young wife and mother. By now she had been away from her family for a little more than six years, during which time she had given birth to two children, lost two, and, at twenty-six, was anxiously pregnant with another. Back in the embrace of her parents and sisters, my mother felt protected, cherished, and relieved, even if only temporarily, of too much responsibility for a woman not far out of her teens.

"*Oy, a ziesser in kup!*" Zaydie exclaimed as he cradled my "sweet head" and nuzzled it with his chin. As I hugged him, I caught a whiff of pipe tobacco in his long graying beard. Bubby scurried up behind him. Tall, with a round middle and thin legs, she appeared to me like a large, blue-eyed bird. Her kisses were noisy, smoochy pecks—one, two, three, four—on my brow. I gave her a big hug, too. When my mother was happy, so was I.

"*Vass ken ich brengen?*" Bubby asked, immediately trying to press something, anything, on us. I shrugged, and within moments she had reached deep into her walk-in closet and pulled out a bag of sweaters from the textile factory where she worked.

"*Tu ohn, es is kalt,*" she said, rubbing her arms to ward off the nonexistent chill. She held up a thick red sweater that would have been outdated had it ever been in fashion in the first place. Ricki and I both ran away before she could reach us.

"Mammeh, das is nisht schein," my mother said, as she rolled her eyes at the offending garment and laughed.

Undeterred, Bubby set the bag aside and retrieved a guaranteed child-pleaser: a box full of stuff that had somehow escaped detection by the internal radar Zaydie had developed to root out Bubby's clutter. Ricki and I took it from her eagerly, and we spent the next hour rummaging through the tangle of scalped dolls, plastic beads, promotional pens, and broken bits of toys.

The adults, meanwhile, settled themselves into the apartment's only common room. The once-grand apartments had been carved up into smaller units, leaving my grandparents with a single space that served as a combined living room, dining room, den, and library; in my mother's youth it was also the High Holidays guest room. When out-of-town relatives came to stay, they slept under the large table in the center. There being no space for a sofa or even an easy chair, that table became the social center of my grandparents' home, always covered with a tablecloth that was itself covered with plates of food.

My mother insists to this day that her mother was a decent cook, if indifferent to the art of presentation. I looked forward to exactly two items that regularly appeared on her menus: her excellent chicken soup with rice, and the dense, chewy honey cookies purchased at Lowin's Bakery. Everything else seemed to have been some leftover scooped out of an ancient coffee jar that had been covered with a square of waxed paper and secured with a rubber band.

Although she may not have been particularly domestic, no one coped better in a crisis than Bubby. When my grandfather had been imprisoned during one of Stalin's purges—accused of "religious propaganda" and "anti-Soviet" activities—my grandmother found work in a garment factory to support herself and her three little girls. Three years later, when the Nazis advanced on Kharkov, Bubby fled with her girls to Uzbekistan and managed to scratch out a living there as well—more successfully, it was said, than Kharkov's male refugees. When my grandparents were finally able to emigrate, one of the two "carry-ons" they were permitted to take with them was my mother. And when they reached Lvov, the suitcase with Bubby's last few household goods was left behind so that Zaydie could take with them an abandoned Torah scroll that he'd found in a shul.

Even if she wasn't the best cook in the world, clearly there were more important things in life.

I was excited about the week ahead. I'd been given a very special role: Miri's backup *shomeres*. According to Jewish custom, for seven days before the wedding, the bride and the groom could venture outside only if accompanied by a guardian who would protect them from mischief-making evil spirits and, ultimately, ensure their safe arrival at the main event. My fourteen-year-old cousin Leah was Miri's primary *shomeres* and I'd been tapped as her backup. While I looked forward to spending time alone with my aunt, I was also a little nervous about my ability to fend off the malevolent forces waiting to pounce. Imagining them as versions of that cute little cartoon devil in the Underwood canned ham television commercials made me less anxious.

Although I was happy about the wedding itself—my mother had sewn a crown of embroidered daisies for me to wear in my hair—

the prospect of a married Miri made me sad. Only thirteen years older than I, she was my number-one aunt, quick with a joke and able to whip up lavish three-layer coconut cakes at a moment's notice. I was not looking forward to witnessing what I expected to be Miri's sudden and depressing transformation from fun young aunt to old married lady. With her husband and then a rapid succession of babies, our relationship would no doubt change, and I worried that she'd have no time left for me.

I actually loved *all* of my mother's sisters, knowing that I could rely on them to feed, comfort, lecture, and coo over me as needed. They were also among the earliest shapers of my worldview. Passionate analyzers of the human condition, two or more Gurewitz sisters in a room was an instant invitation to deep conversations usually conducted over cottage cheese and coffee. I always grabbed a front-row seat during these exchanges, absorbing talk that touched on family history, novels, dieting, movie stars, decorating, cooking, child rearing, fashion, and, inevitably, their mother. I marveled at the ease with which they moved from topic to topic and at the apparently bottomless well of their knowledge. More than that, I sensed I was previewing a version of my future self, a prospect at once deeply appealing and impossibly foreign. I tried to imagine myself as an adult, magically transported into their circle, a bright scarf tied around my head, nursing my mug of Nescafé. Who would be at the table with me? Would I even have anything to talk about by then? Where would my own experience come from? My mother and her sisters seemed so confident of their place in the world, of what was expected of them, while my own thoughts rushed about in an anxious jumble, trying to make sense of what was going on around me. Observing my aunts in their natural habitat, I experienced a vague tug of longing, and even envy. But when it came to inserting my grown-up self into their midst, my imagination failed me. Despite my deep attachment to them, all I saw was blankness.

After supper my father left for the trip back to New Haven and my mother tucked Ricki and me into bed. I was exhausted, but forced myself to stay awake, fascinated by the sounds of the street. Through the open window I listened to the shouts of children playing outside, adults cackling over garbled jokes, the roar of a car engine that momentarily broke up the party. The voices, with their musical lilts and unfamiliar cadences, belonged not to Lubavitchers but to the West Indians, who lived north of Eastern Parkway. They gave me a glimpse into a world far away from my family and New Haven. I knew that if one day I could live in New York, in my very own apartment in a building that looked like a castle, my life would be perfect.

The week passed quickly. My mother, Ricki, and I visited cousins and shopped in the local stores. One afternoon we drove to Natan Borlam Co., a store in Williamsburg that sold the kind of modest clothing for Orthodox girls that was so hard to find outside of Brooklyn. Inside, a maze of narrow rooms was packed floor to ceiling with long-sleeved, high-necked Shabbos dresses and below-the-knee skirts. Most of the other customers were Satmar Hasidim, and they looked as alien to me as I must have appeared to the Lubavitchers just a few miles away in Crown Heights. The Satmar girls wore dark clothes and thick-seamed stockings, and their hair hung down their backs in long braids. Their mothers, in short wigs topped with hats or scarves, and wearing no makeup that I could see, spoke to them in a Hungarian-inflected Yiddish that sounded like another language entirely. I felt relieved, momentarily, to be a relatively worldly Lubavitcher, even if I didn't entirely fit in with the Crown Heights crowd.

Much to my disappointment, Miri was rarely to be seen. Most days she left the apartment around ten in a giddy rush and returned in the early evening with armloads of shopping bags, only to leave again for dinner with her friends. But one morning, when Leah was otherwise engaged, I was finally recruited for *shomeres* service. We were going to Ratfolvi's, in Flatbush, to pick up the *sheitel* that Miri would be required to wear as a married woman. Pulling up to a residential building, we let ourselves into Mrs. Ratfolvi's wig shop/apartment and sat down in the reception area, where four or five women were chatting away on a damask sofa and chairs.

While we waited our turn, I examined the rows of wigs on display: there were various shades of brunette, blonde, and ginger; short, teased bouffants and glamorous, shoulder-length falls; wigs encased in rollers and wigs that were fully styled, needing nothing more than a final shpritz of hair spray. They were set upon Styrofoam heads complete with turned-up noses, high cheekbones, and luscious lips that looked like they could come alive at any moment. I longed to get my hands on a brush and a pair of scissors so that I could create my own visions of tonsorial loveliness. I did this from time to time to my dolls, to my mother's great irritation, and here was a whole wall of victims.

When Miri's name was called, she plunked herself into the salon chair and pulled the silk scarf off her ponytail. I stood as close as I could without getting in the way. From conversations that I'd overheard between my mother and her sisters, I knew that

Mrs. Ratfolvi was considered "the best," and I was eager to watch her at work. The "rat" in her name had led me to expect someone old and unattractive, but she was actually a nicely put-together middle-aged woman.

The receptionist brought over a plastic case about the size of a chubby toddler. In one expert motion, Mrs. Ratfolvi clicked it open, withdrew the fully styled wig on its Styrofoam head without mussing so much as a strand, and held it up for us to admire. It was a deep chestnut, close to Miri's real hair color and cut just a tad shorter. The perky flip at the bottom reminded me of Ann Marie, Marlo Thomas's character in *That Girl*. Mrs. Ratfolvi eased the wig over Miri's head and secured it with a small comb that had been sewn into the front and that she gently pushed into Miri's real hair. She teased the wig a bit at the top and smoothed it down. Then she stood back, lips pursed, to admire her handiwork. I watched Miri's face as she looked at herself in the mirror. She turned her head from left to right, tugged at the front, and then nodded briskly in satisfaction. Mrs. Ratfolvi beamed. I was disappointed. It looked nice enough, but not nearly as beautiful as Miri's own glossy hair. At home, I sometimes played with my mother's old wigs, twirling in front of the mirror like a ballerina. They itched like crazy, but they made me feel glamorous and grown-up. There was a big difference, however, between playing dress-up and having to wear one of those things on your head all day and every day. I'd watched my mother fuss with hers often enough to know they were a pain. It was something I was not looking forward to.

Sunday finally arrived. My mother dressed Ricki and me in matching pink satin gowns and pinned the ribbons of daisies into our hair so the ends flowed down our backs. She was wearing a chartreuse maternity gown borrowed from my father's sister. Her *sheitel,* a big red bubble, flipped up at the bottom like Miri's. With orders not to wrinkle our clothing, we settled ourselves on the bed and watched while she and her sisters got ready. The room smelled of face powder and Chantilly perfume.

Bubby, getting ready in her own bedroom, took a bit longer, but she finally presented herself to her daughters for inspection and to have her lipstick applied. And a few minutes later, Miri emerged from her room. My eyes widened. She was the most beautiful woman I had ever seen, a fairy-tale princess shimmering in lace and tulle. Her hair, on public display for the last time, framed her face with long, graceful ringlets. At the top sat a pearl tiara, and a veil cascaded down her back. I hung back, suddenly shy in front of this dazzling stranger and not wanting her to catch me gaping at her. She rushed out the door in a cloud of whiteness, accompanied by Bubby and Zaydie.

When my parents, Ricki, and I arrived at the Brooklyn Jewish Center, two blocks from my grandparents' apartment, Miri was seated on a tulle-wrapped throne in the grand ballroom, greeting the first well-wishers above the earsplittingly loud festive music. I tried to get close to her, but the crowd was quickly thickening, making it hard to push through. Unnerved, I gave up and clung to my mother, who told me to take my sister and find something to eat at the smorgasbord tables. We happily munched on cake as we watched the room fill up with women in glittering dresses.

All at once, the music turned sad and serious, and the crowd grew quiet. The ballroom doors opened and Tzvi, my uncle-to-be, entered, flanked by his father and Zaydie, each holding a lit taper.

Short and slight, Tzvi wore a *kittel,* a long white ritual robe, over his suit and kept his head slightly bowed. As the three of them approached, the crowd parted to clear a path to the bride, giving me my chance to scoot right to the front. When they reached Miri, Tzvi stepped forward and stared at her for just a moment before covering her face with her veil. I thought of the Bible story I'd learned in school, about Jacob loving Rachel but being tricked into marrying her older sister, Leah, when their father swapped the older for the younger before the veiled bride was brought to the wedding canopy. Would I be a Leah one day, or a Rachel? I wondered. Tzvi, having seen with his own eyes that he'd gotten the right bride, turned around and let himself be led out of the room. Everyone then crossed Eastern Parkway to 770, the main Lubavitcher shul where the ceremony was to be held. I clutched my mother's hand as she edged in close to the chuppah, and through a muffled thicket of satin skirts I heard the murmurings of blessings, the crunch of breaking glass, and then the joyous shouts of "Mazel tov!" as a beaming Tzvi and Miri, now husband and wife, slowly walked back through the crowd, a gauntlet of kisses and mazel tovs.

Back at the hall, after the first two courses were served, the dancing began in earnest, men on one side of a long partition that bisected the dance floor, women on the other. Miri and Tzvi were hoisted onto chairs by their friends, carried around for a bit, and then set down on their appropriate sides. A large circle of women formed to dance around Miri. I tried to keep up as best I could as one woman after another broke out of the circle to dance in the center with her. First Bubby, then Tzvi's mother, then my mother and Miri's other sisters, then her friends and other nieces—each had a turn with the smiling bride. I was growing anxious about my turn—perhaps I'd been forgotten already?—when Miri looked straight at me, pulled me into the center, and hugged me, hard, like she always did.

"Isn't this fun, pumpkin?" she shouted above the music.

"Yes!" I screamed back, and the two of us danced together for a long time, laughing. Perhaps everything was going to be fine.

4

The *Platz*

I have vivid memories of my mother's pregnancy with Ella: her nose wrinkling as she arranged raw chicken in a broiler pan; her new dresses that gathered, just like mine did, in little pleats at the middle of her rib cage; her taut belly, which she encouraged me to touch as she asked "Did you feel it?" over and over until I said yes.

"You have to be married to have a baby, right?" I asked one day. I was in her bedroom, making a design out of the bobby pins she kept on the dresser tray.

"Well, usually, but not always," my mother answered, and went back to smoothing the duvet on her bed. Perhaps she didn't want to lie, or thought we might continue the conversation at another time. At the moment, however, this was very disturbing news. I conjured an image of myself a few years down the road—age eleven or so—clutching a giant, swaddled infant that had come to me out of nowhere, my bad luck. I wondered how I might explain its presence to my parents and considered the humiliation I would feel in front of my friends. As with much of the troubling information that I pieced together during my childhood, I didn't bother asking for clarification. Overconfident in my powers of observation, I simply added it to the list of things to worry about, another piece of kindling to be thrown onto the pyre of anxiety that crackled beneath me.

Ella was born at the end of October. With my mother in the hospital for the week, Ricki and I were cared for after school by Allie, a local woman who babysat for many of the Orthodox families in town and who spent most of the week in my mother's rocking chair, crocheting ponchos for our dolls and sharing horror stories about people she supposedly knew.

"A neighbor of mine was closing her window one day and got her fingers stuck in between the two windowpanes," she said. "Both hands trapped, so there was no way to get herself loose." Allie got up to demonstrate, keeping the index and middle fingers of one hand free to balance her cigarette. "She hung there for three days. Nearly starved to death." She looked back at the two of us to make sure we understood. As I watched her claw at the frame, I mentally sketched my own escape plan.

The morning Ella came home, I stood at the door and watched my mother slowly climb the front steps holding a pastel bundle in her arms. A song from *Sesame Street* popped into my head.

Oh, I've got five people in my family
and there's not one of them I'd swap.

I ran to my mother and she smiled and leaned over to show me my new little sister. We entered the house together, and she set the baby down in the portable crib my father had put together in the sunroom. I moved in to inspect the merchandise. She was beautiful—a perfect cap of black hair, skin soft as silk, impossibly tiny nails—and she smelled yeasty, like my grandmother's freshly baked challah. I let Ella's little hand coil around my finger, and something shifted inside me, a wrenching so sharp it was almost physical. I felt myself shrinking to make room for one more of "us," for this new, luminous creature. I suddenly felt ugly and ungainly, and definitely not cute.

Ricki, who had been the baby for five years, did not cede her position easily. She threw long tantrums, weeping and burying her face in my mother's lap. My mother would stroke her hair and say over and over, "Don't you know how special you are to me?" I wanted to crawl in beside Ricki, but I hung back and tried to make myself useful instead. In short order, I learned how to warm up a bottle in a pan of hot water and prepare rice cereal at just the right temperature and consistency. I mastered the art of diaper changing, slipping a finger between Ella's tender skin and the pin to avoid pricking her, and dipping the soiled cloth in the toilet before tossing it into the pail filled with disinfectant that we placed on our doorstep each week, to be magically cleaned and refreshed by the diaper service. I took pride in my newly acquired skills but I keenly missed my mother's attention.

"Are you helping Mommy with your baby sister?" people asked. I smiled and nodded, but when I fed Ella breakfast in her high chair, I stuffed her mouth so full of scrambled eggs, she'd spit them all out onto the tray. Once, I pinched her hard enough to make her cry.

I turned to my classmates for distraction, spending as many nights as possible with my best friend, Ariella, who had no siblings left at home and enough Barbies to fill a sorority house. We dressed and arranged them until supper, always tuna noodle casserole at my request. For dessert, we each got a cream-filled Ring Ding, which had only recently received a kosher seal of approval and seemed terribly exotic. When her father came home, he'd briefly entertain us with corny jokes and then leave us to our games. At bedtime, the bottom bed of the high-riser in Ariella's room would be pulled out and neatly made up, with a washcloth and a face towel waiting for me. Everything matched. I couldn't believe Ariella's luck.

Ariella's family was Modern Orthodox, to me the ideal level of Jewish observance. I was only seven years old, but I was starting to recognize that despite the many things Ariella and I had in common, our paths would soon begin to diverge just enough to make a big difference one day. We were similar but not the same. She felt at home here, part of a local community, while I would always stand slightly apart from the Modern Orthodox in New Haven. We were Lubavitchers, Hasidic satellites taking instructions from command central in Crown Heights. Yet as an out-of-towner, I didn't feel part of the Crown Heights crowd either—not that I wanted to be. Doubly unsettled, I wished for Ariella's future instead of my own. Eventually, when we became bas mitzvah at age twelve, I would have to wear blouses that covered my elbows, and the only pants I'd be allowed to wear were pajamas. Later, when we married—me first, no doubt—I'd struggle with an itchy, unattractive *sheitel* while Ariella would go to the beauty salon to have her hair styled and dyed champagne blond like her mother's. She would go to college like her older sister, and marry someone who didn't have a beard.

Ariella and I both kept Shabbos, of course—we turned off the television at candle-lighting time, sat down to festive Friday night dinners, walked to shul the next morning in nice clothing, remembered before we left the house to empty our coat pockets so that we wouldn't be carrying anything out into the street. But where I had to walk two miles through unsafe neighborhoods to the Orchard Street Shul and content myself with geriatric congregants and onion Tam Tams, my friends attended the Young Israel synagogue a few blocks from our house, which had games and frosted brownies at the children's service. I asked my father why he couldn't *daven* there. He explained that it was a bad fit.

"The *mechitzah*'s too low, for one thing. All I have to do is pick up my chin"—he demonstrated with a quick upward jerk of his head—"and I'm looking right into the women's section. Plus, we use a different siddur." Lubavitchers use a prayer book that was edited by Rabbi Isaac Luria, a sixteenth-century kabbalist, rather than the more common Ashkenazic siddur. I knew these were important issues for him, but they weren't for me.

Still, I understood that by Crown Heights standards I had it easy. Unlike most of my relatives in Brooklyn, my family actually owned a television set, and I was allowed to go to the movies, where I saw every Disney feature that came out. My parents were also more relaxed on the issue of *Cholov Yisroel.* They let us have "regular kosher" food like Breakstone's Temp Tee Whipped Cream Cheese on our bagels, Hershey's Kisses, cherry bombes from the ice cream truck at the beach. For the strictest Lubavitchers, these treats might as well have been sprinkled with crushed bacon. (My father, keeping to stricter standards, used only *Cholov Yisroel* products himself, which were shipped to us, like our glatt kosher meat, from Brooklyn.) My sisters and I attended a yeshiva that was coed through the eighth grade, with kids from all levels of observance. Indeed, by the time I'd reached third grade, I'd already developed a thoroughly unrequited crush on a particularly cute classmate named Danny Roberts, who, I thought, looked sort of like Bobby Brady.

If the Modern Orthodox life I wanted seemed unattainable, I

led a rich fantasy existence through books. Reading at bedtime or curled up on the couch on Shabbos, I forgot about annoying younger sisters and didn't worry about fitting in with my friends. Books also provided entrée into all sorts of different worlds, allowing me to freely try on alternative lives. My mother, herself a voracious reader, gave us close to carte blanche on subject matter. As a girl, she had walked to the main branch of the Brooklyn Public Library every Friday afternoon, leaving with armloads of books for the week. Her guilty pleasure, she told me, had been the Cherry Ames nurse novels.

My only restrictions were religious—nothing about Jesus, Christmas, and nuns or priests, unless they were persecuting Jews, in which case I would be learning an important lesson about the untrustworthiness of the goyim. That still left me with plenty to pick from during our own weekly trips to Mitchell Library, not to mention what I found on our own bookshelves. I would read almost anything—books about dinosaurs and Indian tribes, biographies of Helen Keller and the Founding Fathers, confounding instruction booklets dug out of my mother's box of Kotex. But I loved novels most: *The Secret Garden, Homer Price,* and *Ramona the Pest* were particular favorites. I read and reread Maud Hart Lovelace's Betsy-Tacy series, relishing the impossibly perfect small-town existence of pre–World War I Minnesota. Betsy Ray lived the life I craved. High-spirited, confident, smart, and popular, she planned to become a writer when she grew up. She and her crowd spent Saturday afternoons skating on the local pond. They warmed up afterward in her family's Hill Street kitchen where her mother had left sandwiches of delightful-sounding roast beef alongside pitchers of milk, a combination that was as awesomely *trayf* as the rest of her blessed existence. (My mother tried to "kosher up" secular culture for us where she could. Her version of the "On Top of Spaghetti" song, eliminating the forbidden combination of meat and cheese, went like this: *On top of spaghetti, all covered with sauce / I lost my poor meatball when somebody coughed.*)

My interests weren't totally secular. We had many Jewish books at home that I loved. My copy of *The Pitzel holiday book*—about a tiny family in a tiny, unnamed country—fell apart from overuse. So did *The Adventures of K'Ton Ton,* about a Jewish Tom Thumb who, among other mishaps, nearly meets an untimely end under a chopping knife in a bowl of raw gefilte fish. By the time I was eight I was steeped in the tribulations of shtetl life—in tales of Bogdan Chmielnicki, the notorious seventeenth-century Cossack whose pogroms spread terror throughout the Jewish communities in the Russian Pale of Settlement, and in stories about the cruel *poretz,* the Polish nobleman who exacts punishing rents from his impoverished Jewish tenants before meeting his comeuppance.

We didn't learn specifically about Hasidism at school, but I managed to glean a greatest-hits version of Hasidic history from my grandparents' old bound volumes of *Talks and Tales,* a popular compilation of stories for children about legendary Hasidic rabbis. Lying on their living-room rug, I spent Shabbos afternoons flipping through pink mimeographed pages, Yiddish on one side and English on the other, taking in the wisdom and wonders of Reb Nachman of Bratslav, the Mezricher Magid, and especially the Baal Shem Tov, the poor orphan who went on to found the Hasidic movement in the early eighteenth century. The Besht, as he was known, brought to illiterate Jews the notion that one could worship God not just through rigorous study but also through fervent and joyful prayer. A humble laborer and itinerant teacher, he was eventually recognized as a scholar and a sage, and developed a devoted following throughout eastern Europe. The great miracles he was said to have performed—illnesses cured, kopeks discovered at the bottom of wheat sacks, heartfelt repentance by the misguided—became the stuff of legend. Long-barren couples would visit the Baal Shem Tov to plead for his blessing and return the following year to introduce their bouncing baby boy. In one story I read, a disciple exclaims, "How wonderful he is! It's hard to believe he was born of a woman." Confused by the sentence, I accidentally dropped the "of." Born a woman? How, I wondered, had he managed the transformation? It took but a small leap to conclude that if the Baal Shem could cross a river on a handkerchief (as recounted in one of the stories I'd come across), who was to say he couldn't morph from a shtetl babushka into a saintly bearded sage? It would certainly make travel easier, I reasoned, not to mention that miracle making appeared to be the province of men.

I absorbed these tales as though they were part of my own family lore. And in a way they were. From reading about a pogrom in Odessa or a miracle in Mezrich, I could trace a direct line to the stories my parents and grandparents told us, about places such as Dakshitz, where my great-great-grandfather Kusya Deitsch cured his child's eye infection with a yellow cream recommended by the Rebbe Rashab, the fifth Lubavitcher Rebbe; Riga, where Nazis rounded up the town's Jews, including my great-grandfather Reb Itche Gurewitz, locked them in a shul, and set it on fire; Kherson, where Reb Itche's son, my Zaydie Tzemach, boarded a train alone to Nevel, eight hundred miles north, in Stalinist Russia, to study at age thirteen in an underground yeshiva; and Zhlobin, where young Sara Karnovsky, my future Bubby Deitsch, skated on the frozen Dnieper like Betsy Ray herself.

I cherished these family stories of "back there" and felt a strange, almost genetic sense of ownership of them, as though they'd been bequeathed to me, like my brown hair and long piano fingers. But these adventures really belonged to my grandparents, my parents, and my aunts and uncles. While I certainly bore the imprint of their lives in the old country—and not just in their religious practice—I sometimes wondered whether all the interesting stuff had already happened to them and passed me by. Secretly, I wanted to be tested by circumstances, too, as they had been.

It's Sunday morning, and my sisters and I are eating breakfast in the kitchen.

"I've got to go in for a few hours," my father announces as he enters the kitchen, holding his car keys, "to check on some things."

My mother scowls. "Going in" means to the plastics factory. During the week, my father came home at seven, in time only for a greeting and a good-night kiss. He'd also worked Sundays ever since I could remember, but lately my mother had gotten him to agree to be at home with us more often. As he stands there looking uncomfortable, I seize my chance.

"Hey, can I come with you, Daddy?" Now it's his turn to frown.

"That's a great idea," my mother says. "Get your coat."

Fifteen minutes later, I bounce out of the front seat of his car—another treat—and wait for him to unlock the door and disable the alarm on the cinder-block structure that houses the factory's front offices. The building itself lay on a desolate industrial stretch of road covered over with marsh grass and rusted metal drums. Above a grimy window reinforced with chicken wire, a small sign reads: DEITSCH PLASTIC, INC. As if to acknowledge its ineffable hold over the family, we just call it "the *platz*" or, if English is your first language, "the place."

Inside, I inhale deeply, taking a strong hit of polyvinyl chloride. The fumes, like fresh paint, smell familial, the male equivalent of Bubby Deitsch's cornflake-encrusted chicken. The office, which my father shares with my zaydie and uncles, is a jumble of furniture purchased for next to nothing at auction: a few metal desks, rollaway chairs, tall gray file cabinets, and, in the center of the room, a conference table covered with a giant sheet of beige Naugahyde. Every surface in the room overflows with "things"— invoice pads, books of vinyl samples, peppermints, office supplies, and promotional knickknacks that arrive in the mail from time to time.

"I've got some work to do," my father says. "Keep yourself busy."

This will not be a problem. While he shuffles a stack of papers, I sift through the clutter as though panning for gold. As long as I'm not too greedy, I know I will be allowed to walk away with a few souvenirs—a colored pen, perhaps, or an illustrated calendar from one of the bigger clients. Once or twice a year, my father would bring home an enormous carton of ugly plastic handbag samples, which, over howls of protest, my mother would force Ricki and me to give to our teachers for Chanukah and end-of-year presents.

Soon my father gets up and opens a door on the far side of the room.

"Want to come?" he asks. I hurry behind him.

Except for the loud buzz of fluorescent bulbs, the factory floor is completely silent. We head toward the Towmotor, a tractor-like vehicle with two steel prongs in front for lifting pallets. I clamber in next to my father, and we ride without talking past hulking gears, conveyor belts, tubs of ink, and, here and there, the canvas jacket of an employee who would bring these machines to life come Monday. And everywhere, there are rolls of vinyl stacked in fat pyramids of brown, black, tan, and—the fashion color of 1971—crinkly white, just like the go-go boots my father had recently brought home for me, another sample.

Zaydie Deitsch had started the business in the mid 1950s, soon after the family arrived from Europe. They settled in Norwalk, Connecticut, where my grandfather had a job waiting for him at a relative's tie factory. Born in 1917, the same year Tsar Nicholas was deposed, he'd always had a knack for making money out of nothing. As a boy in Kharkov, he learned how to turn rubles into francs on the black market and how to melt down celluloid film to make plastic hair combs. Later, he managed to support his extended family by skimming off dyes and yarn from *tricotage,* a type of knitting work that most religious Jews did at home to avoid having to work on Shabbos. As the family moved through the displaced-persons system after World War II and settled in Paris for a time, he pressed grapes into contraband kosher wine to sell to other refugees. Looking around for an opportunity in Connecticut, he found it (a decade before *The Graduate*) in plastics.

New Haven was a logical place for Zaydie to settle. Situated along the Northeast textile corridor, it already had a few

Lubavitcher families and a yeshiva for my aunts. Before the move, Zaydie visited the newly appointed Lubavitcher Rebbe, Menachem Mendel Schneerson, to pledge his fealty and ask for the Rebbe's blessing for the new enterprise.

"I'm your soldier," my grandfather said. "Tell me what you need and I'll get it done."

The Rebbe tasked him with providing financial support to expand the boys' yeshiva in Crown Heights, assuring him that if he did, his business would meet with great success.

The Rebbe's blessing appeared to work. Over the years, my father and uncles were brought into the company. The factory was riding the synthetics wave, and we all drank from a deep, seemingly bottomless well that bound us tightly together. My grandparents bought a small ocean-front condo in Miami Beach and began spending three weeks down there every January, returning home with bronzed complexions and gifts of plastic-wrapped kosher snack cakes saved from the plane. My parents traded in their old Chevette for an Oldsmobile station wagon and added a second car for my mother. Among Lubavitchers, a community of meager resources, we were the Astors of pleather.

My father stops the Towmotor near a stand of vinyl and hops off. Pulling on the end of a roll, he fishes a retractable razor from his shirt pocket and cuts a small square of material, like a geologist taking a core sample. He rubs the fabric between his fingers and examines the woven backing, his expression thoughtful. I wonder what his touch revealed—it seems no different from any of the other rolls we'd passed—but when he climbs back in, I feel too shy to ask. This is his domain, a closed circle shared with the other men in the family. I worry that he might find my curiosity intrusive or, worse, proof of female simplemindedness. Both of my parents expect me to do well at school, but I understand that there is something unfeminine, even unnatural, about women going into business when they don't need to. I would always be taken care of, and stupid questions would only remind my father that I had no place here.

"Can we go home soon?" I ask instead.

In sharp contrast to my mother's side of the family, my father's was an indisputably male tribe. Notwithstanding my parents' expanding clutch of daughters, in the final tally of Deitsch grandchildren, boys would outnumber girls twenty-five to fifteen. Even beyond the numbers, we girls never stood a chance. If Hasidic women were generally expected to keep a low profile, my grandparents had even stricter ideas about appropriate male and female behavior. I learned early that the following activities were deemed dangerously emasculating: clearing the table, food preparation of any kind, dressing a baby, reading a novel, letting a woman finish a sentence without interrupting her. At the same time, a corollary lesson for us girls suggested that while these same activities defined ladylike behavior, they were, in the larger scheme of things, of no great significance. To me, it felt like a sucker's game I couldn't win.

My male cousins ran through my grandmother's pristine house like a pack of unleashed hounds, cutting a swathe of noisy destruction and demanding to be fed. My sisters and I trailed them from a safe distance.

"Kinder!" Bubby would shriek after a sudden crash upstairs. "What's going on?"

My grandfather would cackle, both at the chaos and my grandmother's reaction. Eventually she would shake her head and smile, too. *"Mazik,* don't break my house," she'd say affectionately when the prime offender finally presented himself.

Roughhousing of this sort was simply unthinkable for girls. So was talking back to a grown-up or displaying intelligence that was superior to any boy's, no matter how stupid the boy was. Not wanting to get lectured, I said less and less around my relatives, particularly the men. I couldn't help but feel that there was something inherently shameful about being a girl, like making the best of a bad limp. Being a "woman" was even worse, evoking a feminist creature too full of swagger, too in-your-face for her own good. The very word evoked mysterious bodily effluences, and I could barely utter it without my flesh creeping a bit.

I struggled to square this king-of-the-castle sensibility with the amazing stories I'd heard about the women of my grandmother's and great-grandmother's generations. They'd survived first the Bolsheviks and then World War II, often with their husbands in exile or in prison. My great-grandmother Hinda Deitsch ran a soup kitchen in Tashkent, Uzbekistan, and undertook a mind-boggling thousand-mile journey to rescue her son from a labor camp in Chelyabinsk. *Ach, those were terrible times,* my relatives would sigh as they recounted these fascinating stories, *you should never know from them.* I wondered how these women were able to go back to their sheltered, circumscribed lives after performing what seemed to me acts of almost magical bravery under such difficult conditions.

That was the part of their lives that I wanted: those few years they spent in control of their own destinies, with no men around to make them feel small or useless. Unlike many other little girls, I had never gone through a "bride" phase, with fantasies of a fairy-tale wedding to a handsome prince with whom I'd live happily ever after. Marriage, which from what I'd observed seemed to be simply staying at home with an ever-increasing number of children to take care of, felt like a hopelessly inadequate form of fulfillment, more hindrance than something to aspire to. My Barbies were perpetually single, never even engaged to their dull-looking Kens. While I often took the role of Mommy when we played house, it was only in order to boss the other kids around. What I really wanted was to be "That Girl," whose adventures I breathlessly followed every week on television. I marveled at the trappings of Ann Marie's bachelorette life: her sweetly furnished New York City apartment, the ups and downs of her acting career, her mod wardrobe, her comic timing. It was clear that she would never marry her nice-but-boring fiancé Donald, and that suited her just fine. I didn't know anyone who lived remotely like her, but to me it looked even better than being Modern Orthodox.

What it boiled down to was quite simple: I wanted my own *platz*.

5

Conscientious Objection

As Lubavitchers in New Haven, our shul options were limited to exactly one. Lubavitchers in Crown Heights, on the other hand, could chose from perhaps a dozen *shtieblach,* little shuls that were tucked into small buildings on side streets throughout the neighborhood. Each had its own raison d'être: some catered to families with young children, some were for more "modern" Lubavitcher businessmen, and some were intended for men who wanted to re-create the intensely Hasidic prayer experience of their fathers and grandfathers back in the old country. But the *shtieblach* were mere spokes in a wheel whose hub stretched across a half block on busy Eastern Parkway. Known simply as "770," for the street address, this was the mother ship, a group of buildings that served as a giant shul, central meeting place, offices, space for wedding ceremonies, and the official headquarters of the Lubavitcher movement. It was here that the Rebbe spent virtually all his waking hours, tending to his flock, getting out his message, and meeting with the legions of Lubavitchers and non-Lubavitchers who sought his advice or support.

The exterior of 770, an architectural hodgepodge of what were originally separate structures, gives few clues to the rabbit warren of stairways, rooms, and corridors within. The first building purchased, an elegant Tudor carriage house with the actual 770 address, had been bought in 1940 from a Jewish doctor who ran a medical clinic in which, the story went, he performed backroom abortions. The adjacent real estate was added as the community grew, and interior walls were knocked down to create enormous public rooms. By the early 1970s, the shul at 770 could easily accommodate a thousand or more congregants, men on the cavernous main floor and women a half story up, ringing the men's section behind Plexiglas plates.

Seven seventy always bustled with activity, but never more so than in late September and early October, when in addition to the locals, hundreds of out-of-town Lubavitchers flocked to Crown Heights for the High Holidays. We made the pilgrimage as well, every Rosh Hashanah until I was eleven, when sister number four arrived, making us too large a herd to impose even on relatives.

For that last trip we stayed, as we always did, with Aunt Yocheved and Uncle Zalman, who lived in a large row house a few streets away from Bubby and Zaydie Gurewitz's cramped apartment. We arrived a few hours before sundown to loud greetings and a flurry of instructions on where to put our luggage. My parents, Ricki, and Ella took a downstairs bedroom, while I got to bunk upstairs, as usual, with my cousin Shayna. At fourteen, she was a goddess in my eyes—beautiful, funny, unfailingly kind, an older sister who didn't mind having me around, as I did my own siblings. She had transformed her bedroom into a sanctuary of femininity, with ruffled bed linens and a French-provincial vanity arrayed with perfume bottles and delicate jewelry. Her wardrobe—meticulously maintained blouses, dresses, sweaters, and skirts—was handed down to me, piece by piece, as she weeded out garments that no longer fit her. I loved getting them, although, having rounded out across the middle, I didn't get to wear them for long, either.

I unpacked my things and came downstairs for candle lighting. The men and boys left for shul, giving the women an hour or so to catch up on local chitchat, set the table, lay food out on the platters, and pore through old photo albums. I pulled out a deck of cards— I'd just learned how to play Spit—but my mother stopped me: not appropriate for Rosh Hashanah. Here we go again, I thought. The solemnity of this holiday always turned the adults short-tempered and grim-faced, making me feel sad and inexplicably angry. Even my uncle Zalman restrained himself; there would be none of the usual gossip at the table or postprandial gin rummy tournaments with the kids. Rosh Hashanah, the Jewish New Year, inaugurated the Ten Days of Repentance, our last chance to atone for our sins before Yom Kippur, when Hashem sealed our fate for the year ahead. It was time to get down to the business of repentance.

I was not in a repenting frame of mind. While I liked the visual narrative of the High Holidays—the white-bearded, white-robed deity pondering an oversized ledger full of everyone's good and bad deeds, the gates of repentance slowly creaking closed— I couldn't connect it to my individual peccadilloes. Certainly I had misbehaved during the year; I talked back to my parents, yelled at my sisters, excluded a classmate from a game. But that was between the injured party and me. Surely Hashem was much too busy thinking up punishments for the real sinners—the terrorists who'd killed the Israeli athletes in Munich, for example, or the airplane hijackers whose pictures I'd seen in *Time*—to concern Himself with my small-scale transgressions. Besides, I wouldn't be officially responsible for my misdeeds until my bas mitzvah, which was two years away. For now, any bad things that I'd done were still charged against my parents' account with God. And it was their judgment I worried about more than God's. At the moment, however, my concerns were more mundane: how I was going to survive the endless services over the next two days.

I woke up the next morning with my stomach in knots. *Davening* started at ten, but my mother and aunt took their time getting ready, lingering over their coffee before getting dressed. We left Ella with a sitter and departed at ten thirty, greeting along the way the few other stragglers hurrying past us. The day was unexpectedly warm, and as we picked up our pace I felt myself overheating in my new dress and tights. I wondered how I could avoid going to the bathroom until the services ended at three o'clock. The local girls tended to hang out in packs near the sinks and managed the neat trick of both ignoring and staring at me as though I had sprouted a beard or a third eye.

The one thing that didn't worry me was where we would sit. Like many shuls, 770 raised money by selling seats for the High Holidays, and every year we rushed to reserve our prime spots— first row in the women's section, with a guaranteed view of the Rebbe. We opened the door of the women's section to face a murmuring forest of dresses and heels. Aunt Yocheved, battle-ready, took the lead, scything through row after dense row of humanity without so much as an "excuse me" or apologetic shrug. We finally reached the front and squeezed past two women who, sighing and shaking their heads at our lateness—today of all days—were forced to stand up and hug their prayer books against their chests to let us through. My grandmother was already there, immersed in prayer, holding her *machzor* inches from her face to make out the tiny type. She looked up, startled, when Yocheved tapped her on the shoulder.

"*Mammeh, gut yontif,*" Aunt Yocheved said, simultaneously hugging and nudging her mother further down the long wooden bench. Our reserved spaces, each measuring roughly twelve inches across, were marked by four white stickers with DEITSCH scribbled on them in Hebrew. But with children included there were actually six of us, with one or two more cousins expected to stop by later. Somehow we would shoehorn the youngest girls onto laps or wedge them upright against someone's knees. Easing a hip between my mother and Shayna, I thought of the story we'd just learned in school, of the ancient Holy Temple in Jerusalem on festival days, when the entire population of Israel miraculously fit into the main sanctuary. I looked around to get my bearings and spotted the Roginsky twins across the aisle. Two years ahead of Shayna at school, they lived in my grandparents' apartment building and made a striking pair, tall and big-boned, with straight black hair and olive skin. As someone extremely protective of my own identity, I was fascinated by their double-ness. I watched with great interest as they whispered the *davening* with intense concentration, bowing and twisting meditatively from side to side, in perfect sync.

I scanned the men's section below, marveling as always at the massive pit of swaying black hats and white prayer shawls. Young men and boys crowded onto bleacher seats that sagged alarmingly under their weight. They literally spread up the wall, as though pinned by some invisible force. Every so often an avalanche would send a few of them cascading down, miraculously with no harm done.

Directly beneath us, my father stood shoulder to shoulder with his father, brother, several cousins, and a jumble of little boys I didn't recognize. From where I was sitting, on the wrong side of the Plexiglas partition, I envied the children who frolicked around him like puppies. He looked up at the darkened window, and my mother stuck her fingers through a thin gap in the partition and wiggled them. He smiled and went back to his *machzor.*

"Can you see?" my mother asked. She meant the Rebbe. He *davened* on a platform in the right front corner, so I pressed my left cheek against the partition. Squinting through one eye, I could just make out a sliver of the back of his head, which was covered by his tallis. I nodded.

I tried to keep up with the *davening*—it helped pass the time for one thing—but the hazan sped through most of the prayers, slowing down only for the crowd favorites. When it came time to sing *Attah B'chartanu,* a wave of excitement rippled through the men's section. I heard the shuffle of leather soles behind me as women and girls edged in closer to try to see. Shayna rose and pressed her thin body against my back, arms draped about my shoulders like a shawl. A girl quickly stepped onto her vacant seat, stretched herself over our heads, and braced a palm against the partition, which bent outward under the pressure.

"Look!" Shayna breathed.

This time I really could see him. The Rebbe had turned to face the congregation. Framed by the tallis that covered his head, his face seemed to glow as he took in the room. The place grew strangely silent, as though time had stopped. The Rebbe lifted his arm and made slow, wide arcs with his fist. As he did so, the men began to sing the traditional Rosh Hashanah melody, louder and louder. The sheer volume of it sent shock waves through the room and shivery chills up my spine. No matter how many times I'd witnessed this scene, it never failed to overwhelm me.

No one had ever sat me down and explained the Rebbe to me— who he was, what he meant to us, or even what his given name was. He was simply the Rebbe and he had always been here, or, rather, had hovered just offstage as we went about our lives. If Hashem was the playwright who conjured up everything that happened in the world, we believed the Rebbe was his favorite director, blocking our moves and interpreting the script for our Lubavitcher troupe. My father, like most Lubavitcher men, kept a picture of the Rebbe in his wallet, alongside snapshots of his children.

The Rebbe's primary role was to provide his followers with spiritual nourishment and guide them to better serve Hashem. He delivered complex discourses on Hasidic teachings and philosophy at *farbrengens,* mass gatherings that occurred throughout the year. He spoke, in Yiddish and without notes, for hours, breaking from time to time to allow for vigorous singing by the crowd. The Deitsch men—my father, grandfather, and uncles—would drive into Crown Heights to *farbreng* with the Rebbe on the major Lubavitch celebration days: the nineteenth of Kislev, when the Alter Rebbe, Rabbi Shneur Zalman of Liadi, the founder of Lubavitch Hasidism, was released from a St. Petersburg prison; the twelfth of Tammuz, the birthday of the sixth Rebbe; and the tenth of Shevat, the day he died. (Hasidim celebrate the anniversaries of a person's death because it is believed that the soul ascends to a higher level of heaven with each passing year.) *Farbrengens* usually began in the early evening and ended around midnight with the men lining up to receive, directly from the Rebbe, small plastic shot glasses of wine for drinking a *l'chaim*. My father would save his, pouring it carefully into a pill bottle he'd brought from home. The following Shabbos, he would mix it with the kiddush wine on Friday night, so we could all share it and, by extension, share in his personal interaction with the Rebbe. While my little sip of Rebbe wine tasted no different than the usual kiddush wine, drinking it somehow made me feel different, like I'd just taken some medicine and was now waiting for it to take effect.

Every Lubavitcher family owned a set of bound transcriptions of the Rebbe's talks, meant to be read, debated, and studied alongside the Torah and Talmud. On winter Saturday nights, when Shabbos ended early, my father would meet with a group of local men to study for a few hours; on the nights he hosted, my mother baked one of her glazed walnut chiffon cakes. By the mid-1970s, *farbrengens* were transmitted live from 770 through special telephone lines, and my father's group would gather in the kitchen to hear the Rebbe on a speakerphone. They listened with rapt attention, but I couldn't follow a word of the Rebbe's Yiddish, and no one translated for me.

The community looked to the Rebbe to fill more mundane needs as well, consulting him on business matters, as well as seeking blessings for marriages, surgeries, and other major life events. Requests were usually telephoned in to his office and, unless they were urgent, answered in written form, dictated by the Rebbe and typed up by one of his male secretaries. No wedding, graduation, bar mitzvah, or fund-raising dinner officially got under way until the host read aloud a personal letter of congratulations from the Rebbe, first in the original Hebrew and then translated into English. These letters became talismans in and of themselves, carefully stashed away with life insurance policies and birth certificates.

My own relationship with the Rebbe was at some remove. Despite their deep reverence for him, my parents left my sisters and me to absorb his teachings on our own. Stories about the Rebbe and his six predecessors, as familiar to other Lubavitcher children as "Little Red Riding Hood" or "Chicken Little," came to us from storybooks or from visitors to our Shabbos table who wanted to share some of the Rebbe's teachings on the Torah. If my parents mentioned him at all, it was in the context of people they knew who had "written in," signaling to me that an engagement or hospital stay was imminent. Perhaps they didn't realize the depth of our ignorance, or assumed that we'd pick up our Hasidic education at school. In fact, neither the Rebbe nor the *Tanya*—the book containing the central guide to Lubavitcher philosophy—made it into our curriculum. Without anyone meaning for it to happen, our formal Lubavitch education slipped through the cracks.

I saw the Rebbe less as a concrete person, or even a beacon for my spiritual and daily life, than as a constant, vague presence. He was not as remote as the president, not as intimate as a relative, but he was someone important who knew my family from way back. That he had miracle-making powers I never doubted. Miracles were to holy men what pirouettes were to ballerinas; it was simply what they did. My mother said he had once read her mind. When she and my father had become engaged, they were granted a *yechidus,* a rare private audience with the Rebbe. Having conferred his wishes for a happy, fruitful, and committed Hasidic marriage, the Rebbe turned to my mother, shook a finger at her, and said, "Do not wear makeup on Shabbos. And tell your friends the same."

She was stunned. Most types of makeup were forbidden on Shabbos—their use fell under the rule that prohibited painting on the Sabbath—but many Lubavitcher women couldn't resist a light application of lipstick before leaving the house. My mother had always gone barefaced, but she sorely missed her lipstick when she got dressed for shul. Now that she'd secured a match and was a bit less worried about angering God, she'd secretly planned to join the ranks of makeup wearers—until the Rebbe had called her out on it. His admonishment certainly had a lasting impact: I had never known to her to cheat.

I took this episode and others like it to heart, seeing them as cautionary tales about the perils of meeting the Rebbe face-to-face. Although he was said to love children, I felt sure that as soon as he laid eyes on me, his kindly smile would fade into a scowl. He would see clear through to my blackened, decade-old soul. Like a perp in a lineup, I would be called out for an alarming and shameful catalog of sins, among them talking back to my mother, bullying my sisters, sneaking nonkosher candy at the doctor's office, falling in love with Pete from *The Mod Squad*.

So when my mother told me one spring day when I was ten that our family was having a *yechidus* with the Rebbe the very next Sunday, I panicked.

"I don't want to go," I said.

"What are you talking about? It's a great honor," she said. "We're very lucky to get the appointment."

"I'm afraid."

"There's nothing to be afraid of. He'll probably just ask your name and you'll tell him. Then Daddy will ask him for a *brachah* for the whole family, he'll give it, and we'll be done. Ten minutes at the most."

It had never occurred to me that I might have to speak. That terrified me even more.

"No," I said.

"We'll talk about it later."

All week, I tried to think of ways to get out of having to meet the Rebbe. I hinted at a stomachache that threatened to worsen. I mentally sacrificed first my grandmother, then my sisters; a funeral or grave illness would surely postpone the trip. And as we loaded into the car on Sunday morning, I prayed for engine trouble. Traffic to New York was unusually light that day.

In the end, I pitched a fit right in front of 770, weeping and begging not to go even as my father parked the car. My tantrum both mystified and exasperated him.

"What's your problem?" he demanded. "How could you be afraid of the Rebbe? He loves you."

"I don't know, I just am," I sobbed, my chest heaving in great waves, my eyelids puffed to slits. I felt humiliated crying in the street and furious at Ricki's nonchalance, but the idea of having my foibles unmasked was more than I could bear.

My parents finally relented, leaving me to wait in the cement yard in front of the shul. I leaned against a brick wall and watched men dash in and out of the swinging doors that led to the main shul, like waiters at a busy restaurant. Clusters of young boys lingered nearby, laughing and chattering in Yiddish. Here and there, young couples stood together quietly, waiting to see the Rebbe. I didn't envy them. Safely out of range of his all-knowing gaze, I knew I had been spared a terrible fate.

Although I managed to dodge that particular face-to-face, the Rebbe's image was an inescapable presence in our house. It was around this same time that my parents purchased a large oil portrait of the Rebbe, a common feature in Lubavitcher households. It had been painted by Hendel Lieberman, the community's sanctioned Rebbe portraitist. Hendel, a distant relative on my father's side, had studied at the Leningrad Secondary Art School and was rumored to have met Marc Chagall. While lacking the dreamy beauty of a Chagall, our painting did have an otherworldly, off-kilter feel to it. The background, thick smears of blue, black, and white, practically vibrated off the canvas, making the Rebbe appear to leap out of it. Rendered from the shoulders up, the portrait showed him from about a decade earlier, in his mid-sixties, a man just beginning to bow under the weight of age. But the piercing blue eyes, from which emanated a bottomless intelligence and, as I well knew, an X-ray gaze with mind-reading abilities, were those of a person who existed beyond conventional boundaries of time and space. The Rebbe's black clothing—a snappy fedora and double-breasted Hasidic *kapota*—seemed flat and one-dimensional by contrast, as if his face had sucked up all of the life on the canvas.

My parents debated where to hang it. The living room would offer the most visibility, but my mother liked to read on the sofa and would have felt awkward putting her feet up in front of the Rebbe. It certainly could not go in the den, where we kept the television. They settled on the dining room, which we used almost exclusively for Shabbos and holiday meals, reasoning that our behavior there would occasion the least disrespect. My usual seat faced the wall on which my parents hung the portrait, and while the Rebbe eventually melded into the rest of the room, I spent our first few months together guiltily avoiding his penetrating scrutiny.

But even as I pulled away from the Rebbe, he was rallying the community around a new and highly public mission, one that would make Chabad—the acronym that served as an alternative name for the Lubavitcher movement—and Chabad Houses fixtures on college campuses throughout America and in locales as far away as Bangkok and Kazakhstan. In 1973, the year I turned ten, the Rebbe kick-started his program of *mivtzo'im,* religious campaigns rolled out with military precision and aimed at capturing the hearts and minds of unaffiliated Jews throughout the world.

The goal of the *mivtzo'im,* we were told, was to hasten the arrival of the Moshiach, the Messiah; the more unobservant Jews we were able to get to take on at least one religious practice, the faster he would come. Belief in the Messiah was neither new nor specific to Lubavitchers, of course. One of the basic tenets of Jewish faith was that at some point during our current exile God will send into our midst a man who will lead us all back to the Holy Land, rebuild the Temple, and usher in an eternity of peace and righteousness. But where most observant Jews were content to go about their daily business while they waited, Chabad went a step further in trying proactively to expedite the process.

We'd learned about Moshiach in school, although our teachers seemed hazy on the details. What I gleaned was this: After he arrived, sin would come to an end, all Jews would become observant, and the entire world would acknowledge the existence of God. We'd all move to Israel, including the deserving dead, who would roll underground to the Holy Land and emerge, resurrected, in Jerusalem. We were warned, though, that resurrected bodies would incorporate only those parts that had been buried in the ground, so if you had been foolish enough to have yourself intentionally cremated, you would most definitely not be included. Based on this information, the Messianic age seemed dull at best, frightening at worst, and only raised more questions. How good did you have to be in order to qualify for resurrection? What would happen to my grandfather's friend, Charlie Bloom, who'd lost a leg to diabetes and went about on crutches? What would our new life in Israel look like? Would there be electricity, or even cars? The vision of my father navigating our Pontiac through narrow Jerusalem streets didn't seem very realistic. It seemed more reasonable to incorporate myself into biblical Jerusalem as depicted in my mother's needlepoint that hung in the living room. I'd be one of the robed women carrying an urn on her head, walking alongside a donkey cart. As for what we'd do once we got there, the truly righteous would learn Torah all day, we were told. The rest of us, I supposed, would have to wait until we got there to find out.

The implementation of the Rebbe's Moshiach campaign was swift and life changing. Seemingly overnight, Lubavitcher men, women, and children were expected to approach perfect strangers and pry into their religious lives.

"Excuse me, are you Jewish?"

A "no" was met with a disappointed but polite "Well, have a nice day." A "yes" set the cogs in motion. Like Fuller Brush salesmen, we were equipped with official accessories, samples of just the right mitzvahs to meet our clients' needs. A glossy pamphlet explained that there were six basic precepts that even a Jew who was new to observance could undertake: lighting Shabbos candles (for women and girls over three), donning tefillin (for men and boys over bar mitzvah), hanging a mezuzah on your doorpost, studying Torah, giving money to charity, and keeping Jewish holy books in your home. Carloads of women hit the local malls, handing out neatly bagged kits containing a metal candleholder, a standard Shabbos candle, and a calendar containing the local Shabbos candle-lighting times. Mitzvah tanks—giant Winnebagos filled with yarmulkes, charity boxes, and pleasantly determined, earnest young men in their late teens and early twenties—began rolling through the streets of Manhattan and other large urban areas throughout the United States, crackling out tinny recordings of old Hasidic tunes from roof-mounted speakers. A mitzvah tank even drove through downtown New Haven before the major holidays.

At summer camp, I dutifully sang the ditties that helped us memorize the list of mivtzo'im.

(To the tune of "Frère Jacques")
I have a mezuzah, I have a mezuzah
On my door, on my door
And now I'm gonna tell you
And now I'm gonna tell you
What it's for.

To kiss the mezuzah, to kiss the mezuzah
Is my aim, is my aim
For on it is written

For on it is written
Hashem's name.

This was a baby's song, of course—what middle-schooler didn't
know what to do with a mezuzah?—but we learned the entire
repertoire with the understanding that one day we'd pass it on to
those less schooled than we were. Mezuzah-wise, I was not a particularly diligent practitioner, constantly forgetting to touch the
little parchment-filled case affixed to the doorpost when I passed
through our front door, and then press my fingers to my lips. But
even if I had been a passionate and fervent mezuzah kisser, I would
have kept it to myself. The whole outreach business seemed a little
crazy to me, and embarrassing, just one more thing that set me
apart from my New Haven friends. Deep down, too, I recognized
the hypocrisy of urging someone else to be a better Jew while I
failed to follow my own advice.

My parents were barely more comfortable than I was with the
idea of proselytizing. By now, they had been away from Crown
Heights for more than a decade and had adapted to their Yankee
surroundings by keeping as low a profile as their appearance would
allow. They had also grown accustomed to a more lenient religious
lifestyle. They were friendly with the local Modern Orthodox
families and no longer worried about getting "caught" going to
the movies. The idea of pressing onto others their own religious
ideology—no matter how deeply they personally believed—sat
badly with them, violating my mother's sense of propriety and
touching a libertarian nerve in my father. He could opt out,
using work as an excuse, but my mother was known to be available during the day. She made a few halfhearted attempts to do

her part but it was a doomed endeavor, like trying to teach a cat how to drive. Standing at the entrance to the local ShopRite and exhorting harried housewives to send their children to Jewish day schools tapped into one of her greatest fears—appearing ridiculous in public. Each time she came home slightly shell-shocked, as though she'd barely survived a hazing.

The type of Lubavitch Hasidism my parents had known as children was hardening into something more rigid and judgmental. Back then, in the 1950s, physically and spiritually traumatized from the war and simply trying to find their footing in their new country, the community had more pressing things to worry about than the spiritual lives of other Jews. Religious standards were more relaxed. Women of my mother's generation were not criticized for wearing their kerchiefs with an inch or two of hairline exposed. Families were smaller, with seven or eight offspring being the exception and not the rule.

But this was all changing. Now, self-appointed *tznius* monitors made sure that, as the Rebbe's representatives, our standard of female modesty was up to snuff. For the girls, that meant stricter adherence to the dress codes and lectures at school on the primacy of a Jewish woman's inner beauty and her spiritual superiority to men, both of which needed to be protected like precious flowers. For the married ladies, shame and the fear of inspiring gossip did the trick. Hairlines went back under wraps and sleeves descended well below the elbow; the stocking-less ankle became a rare sight. There was a song for this, too.

(To the tune of the "Colonel Bogey March," or the march from the movie *The Bridge on the River Kwai*)

Tznius! That is our battle cry!
Tznius! It's what we do or die!
Tznius, cover your knee-us,
Cover your shoulders, your elbows, your thighs.

The roster of *mivtzo'im* continued to expand. In short order we also learned songs about eating kosher and about "family purity"; that is, the Jewish laws governing marital intimacy, which made me blush even though I wasn't completely sure what they were talking about. Growing increasingly resentful of his power over us, I began fantasizing about a Rebbe-less existence. In one scenario, the Rebbe has a Godly revelation instructing him to cancel the observances I personally found too constraining: not wearing pants, wearing only long-sleeved blouses, and covering my hair when I got married chief among them. In another version, only slightly more far-fetched, my Lubavitcher life is actually a dream, and if I could just figure out how to wake myself up—intense concentration, leg pinching, vigorous eye rubbing—I would awaken to my own personal Messianic era: one in which Crown Heights was simply a neighborhood in Brooklyn and men didn't get whiskey-happy at the Shabbos table and sing so loudly that no one could talk; a paradise in which I could wear whatever I wanted, go to college, and get married in my twenties rather than my teens, to a handsome man of my own choosing. I would not feel ashamed of being a girl. Spiritually, there would only be Hashem, invisible and far away, with no holy man who could turn your life upside down with just a nod or a shake of the head. There would be no Winnebagos, no brochures. I could finally be what I'd always dreamed of: Modern Orthodox, like my friends in New Haven.

These imaginings allowed no room for the possibility that my parents might have been just as religious even without the Rebbe (there were a great many ultra-Orthodox Jews who were not Lubavitch, after all) or—a thought even more *trayf* than wishing for a Rebbe-less existence—that one day I could simply choose to leave the entire Orthodox world. It was far easier and much less threatening to make the Rebbe the catalyst of my discontent. Here was an authority figure formidable enough to keep me bound to a tradition that had begun to chafe, yet distant enough to be able to abandon when the time came.

6

Discovering Gloria

My friend Jordana and I scaled the mound of snow piled up at the curb, our winter boots sinking into soft white fluff with each step. We'd gotten more than a foot the night before, but by late morning the streets had been cleared enough for the city buses to run. We'd taken advantage of the day off to head to the mall. These unchaperoned shopping expeditions were new; now that we were twelve, our mothers felt that the two of us could handle the short ride downtown. My father had given me twenty dollars, with a warning to bring back change.

The bus rumbled down Goffe Street, past brightly painted housing projects. I noted the backside of the municipal jail; I'd read that people visiting prisoners were often mugged on their way back to their cars. Ten minutes later we rode past a part of town that was forbidding in a very different way: the Yale campus, an imposing Gothic fortress of dark brick. Through a gate marked DURFEE HALL, I glimpsed a snowy quad crisscrossed with freshly shoveled paths. The students inside seemed to move with great purpose—the elite of the elite, I'd been told. It was a world as foreign to me as the public housing projects.

We got off in front of the Green and made our way into the Chapel Square Mall, the twenty dollars in my purse practically begging to be spent. As I entered adolescence, my acquisitive gene, inherited no doubt from Bubby Gurewitz, came spectacularly to life. It was not, in my case, overcompensating for a life of privation, just some psychic hole that needed to be filled with stuff. I couldn't stop buying things, whether it was shopping at the mall, picking up souvenirs during class trips, or sending away for stamps of the world or trick glasses that were advertised in the backs of magazines. Collections of international dolls and small glass animals were arrayed in artful clusters on my bookcase shelves. A large dresser drawer was dedicated to a jumble of hair accessories, lip gloss, eye shadow, soap samples, and other beautifiers that multiplied like fungus. My jewelry box—an old one of my mother's that I'd re-covered in pink velvet—sparkled like a pirate's chest with cheap rings, necklaces, earrings, and pins. Why buy one thing when you could have four?

I came by my shopaphilia honestly, and not just from my grandmother. My mother was on a constant lookout for sales. The two of us often pulled into Shoe World on the way home from orthodontist appointments to see if anything new had come in, and now that I'd moved into ladies' dress sizes, she had begun carrying out her maternal duty of training me in how to "do" Loehmann's. Forced to try on outfit after outfit in the common fitting room, I learned that "sometimes a dress can look lousy on the rack, but fabulous when you put it on" and, after she'd paid for our purchases at the cash register, that "you always find the best stuff on the way out of the store." Having grown up poor, my mother had made do as a girl with hand-me-downs from cousins or with whatever Bubby Gurewitz found for her at the local shul bazaar. She'd never forgotten the sight of frilly new dresses laid out on the bed of a wealthy friend, and often my sisters and I came home from school to find a skirt or some socks, their tags attached, neatly folded on our coverlets.

"Let's start at Casual Corner," I said to Jordana. "I need earrings."

"Sure," Jordana said. She was essentially along for the ride. She used her own babysitting money for shopping and was saving hers for a cone at Baskin-Robbins.

Inside the store, I slowly turned the display on the countertop carousel, scrutinizing the display of shiny earrings. Nothing too big or spangly, or my mother wouldn't let me wear them. I finally narrowed my selection to a pair of large orange hoops and owl-shaped studs with rhinestone eyes. I held up both for Jordana.

"I think the owls are really cute," she said.

Turning to the mirror, I held each option against an ear and pictured what I could wear it with and what it would broadcast to the world about me. A jeweled owl said feminine yet whimsical; hoops were sexy, grown-up. I wrestled with which persona might make me happier. Like everything processed through my adolescent neuroses, the wrong choice, no matter how inconsequential, would lead to sorrow later on.

"Yeah," I finally said, "but I've got more that matches with the hoops."

Halfway into seventh grade, I had already experimented with a number of looks, each laboriously thought out and assembled. Anything worn during the week needed to mesh at least somewhat with our school uniforms of white button-down shirts and gray plaid skirts. A brief flirtation with high-necked *Little House on the Prairie* blouses quickly shifted to "fifties coed," achieved with an old pink sweater of my mother's, Bass saddle shoes, and bobby socks, and then I moved on to a bright-red satin baseball jacket, which constituted a statement all on its own. For now, I had settled on a more eclectic look of athletic jackets, argyle socks, clogs, and, up at the top, a mass of tight curls, which I forced into being by sleeping every night on half a dozen uncomfortable pink foam curlers. Shabbos was more formal—colorful dresses, tan pantyhose, and my first foray into heels. But it was with my Sunday clothes that I was able to express what I felt was the most "me": calico peasant dresses and long denim skirts, the first of perhaps two dozen that I would come to own over the next decade. Although my classmates and I all circled around the same trends, I prided myself on my novel flourishes, gleaned from *Teen* magazine, which I read each month from cover to cover—a red bandanna twisted into my hair, an olive-drab canvas book bag from the Army Navy store, a silver peanut that hung from a chain around my neck, purchased by Bubby Deitsch in a moment of whimsy. Conspicuously absent from any of my ensembles, of course, were pants of any sort. Like Cinderella's gown, they had disappeared at the stroke of twelve, when I became bas mitzvah.

Absorbed by my appearance and by how I "presented" to the world, I spent more and more time alone in my room, with the door locked against the unwanted intrusions of my sisters. I holed up there after supper to do homework, read my novels, model shoes in the mirror, brood about friends, and experiment with new hairstyles and with lip gloss and pale eye shadow—the only makeup I was allowed to wear. I devoted significant hours to fantasizing about boyfriends named David or Joel, handsome composites of film stars, visitors encountered at friends' houses, young men I noticed at bar mitzvahs, or even strangers who'd caught my eye. Invariably, my beau was solidly Modern Orthodox, complete with a small, brightly colored crocheted yarmulke that included his name along the border in a contrasting color. In these vignettes we held hands and sometimes kissed, or sat on a bench and laughed. Not wanting to upstage him, I usually gave him the better lines.

These imaginary relationships were a balm to the torch I still carried for Danny Roberts. We had been classmates since nursery school, but we'd never developed a friendship or even any sort of casual banter. He had always been sweet and shy, with large blue eyes and black hair, and now he'd grown tall and sinewy. I couldn't stop staring at him in class, my heart fluttering, until he turned my way and I blushed. We had little in common. A math whiz, he fared miserably in most other subjects, particularly religious studies; after nine years in yeshiva, he still stumbled over simple Hebrew vocabulary. His yarmulkes alternated between recycled blue satin skullcaps snagged from a bin near the auditorium and the official version made from the same plaid as the girls' uniforms—both sure signs of someone to whom religious observance did not come naturally. Danny's father owned a news shop, giving him access to a seemingly endless supply of comic books and purple gum that he'd chomp on until the principal noticed and made him deposit it in his handkerchief. He had no sense of humor that I could tell, yet I looked for excuses to talk to him, cadging a piece of Bubble Yum or asking for help solving math problems. At recess I lingered at the edge of the boys' kickball games, hoping he'd look at me after a particularly good shot. I scrambled to sit next to him at assemblies. While he was unfailingly polite and did not seem irritated by my presence, it was clear that I—and every other girl in the class, for that matter—could suddenly disappear without diminishing his social circle.

I had to deal instead with the humiliating attentions of Michael Fisher. In fourth grade Michael had taken it upon himself to coach the class on the proper usage of four-letter invectives. He now assumed the role of class pornographer, drawing accomplished Rubenesque nudes on the blackboard and jumping on any off-color double entendre. His jokes about "coming to school" went completely over my head, and it became impossible to use words like "but" or even "as" around him without triggering a snicker. Michael's brain, like Danny's, was a Hebrew-free zone. Unable to master the guttural, he took to addressing me as "Kaya, my love" and would skip around my desk singing "Chu-Chi Face," from *Chitty Chitty Bang Bang,* as my cheeks flushed beet red.

My lovey, lovey, dovey little teddy bear
You're the apfel strudel of mine eye.

My mother was privy to none of this. While I kept few secrets from her, the subject of boys, let alone sex, never came up between us. I had been too embarrassed even to ask her to buy me a training bra the year before, something I desperately wanted. Instead, I moped and wept for days. When she asked me what was wrong, I insisted I didn't know, and it was only by some miracle of maternal intuition that two training bras appeared on my bed one day. My attachment to my mother was deep but uneasy, resting on my belief that there could be no graver sin, in my mind, at least, than transferring my love from her to someone else. It would be the ultimate betrayal.

Not that I gave her an easy time of it. I had no compunction about talking back when she forbade me to go out, or muttering about "slave conditions" when she asked me to bring up laundry from the basement. I was perfectly willing to risk an explosion— a rare but fearsome occurrence—if it meant that I would in the end get my way. These provocations felt forgivable, wiped clean by volunteering to clear the table or babysit so my parents could go out. For me, the real transgressions were those that might damage my ties to her: anything having to do with sex, of course, but also anything that aspired to an existence that took me beyond her very circumscribed world. An independent life, even as I craved it, would mean a rejection of everything that seemed to matter to her. My mother and I were both easy weepers, but it was she who had always seemed a little delicate, she who needed protecting. And perhaps she did. That she was a thirty-one-year-old mother of three, that it was 1975 and a time of social upheaval, for women in particular, or that she might feel unfulfilled or lonely were outside my ken. Those were her unmentionables. All I knew was that it felt safer to keep thoughts about my future to myself—safer for our relationship and safer for my plans, whatever they might be. And so certain subjects were just never discussed.

I entered eighth grade determined to capture some male attention. This was our last year of coed classes. Once we graduated, the non-Orthodox kids would leave for secular high schools that were more focused on getting them ready for college, and our yeshiva high school was for girls only. With no time to waste, I transferred my amatory campaign from Danny to Seth, the only Orthodox boy in our class and, on paper at least, the embodiment of my imaginary sweetheart: handsome, with unblemished olive skin and thick black hair topped by the requisite crocheted yarmulke. The middle of three brothers, he was a good student and well mannered. His parents steered clear of the usual factional scuffles among the various synagogues in town and my parents knew and liked them. Although my having a boyfriend was off-limits, they liked Seth. This was, of course, one serious strike against him. Another was that he wasn't Nick Nolte, who made my blood race that year as young Tom Jordache in *Rich Man, Poor Man,* and whose pictures I diligently clipped and pasted into a scrapbook I kept hidden in my closet. I had devoured both the novel and the TV series, and Tom—the vulnerable tough guy, with a hank of blond hair swept across his forehead—was simply irresistible. But Nick Nolte was in Hollywood and Seth was just a few rows away in class. And he did have that great hair. With Danny obviously a lost cause, I now found myself unable to stop thinking about Seth.

Seth's family lived around the corner from ours, and as the other boys in our class did not live within walking distance, he had to content himself on Shabbos afternoons with the company of nearby female classmates. Our group usually spent the day migrating from house to house, hanging around in living rooms for hours at a time playing Spit or Hearts. Hopelessly outnumbered, often by six to one, Seth learned to tolerate our chatter about shoes and hair, using the time to concentrate on the cards or the treats our mothers would set out. Every once in a while, the father of the house would poke his head in and give Seth a sympathetic nod. Now I began looking for ways to keep him entertained, cutting short our fashion talk or forcing him to participate by pinning my barrettes into his hair, a humiliation he accepted with surprisingly little complaint. I made sure to flop next to him on the couch or, during the week, sit next to him on the school bus, eliciting bemused glances from some of the older high school girls. Seth seemed to find me good company but transmitted no signal that I was anything more to him than a Shabbos stopgap acquaintance. This was much harder work than I'd imagined.

Although boys and shopping had colonized a large portion of my mental attention, I managed to save some space for more cerebral pursuits. I naturally gravitated toward English, acing vocabulary tests and writing thoughtful book reports on *To Kill a Mockingbird, Jane Eyre, Death Be Not Proud,* and other junior high staples. An avid consumer of the news—a legacy, perhaps, of my childhood Cronkite dinners with Zaydie Deitsch—I was also partial to history and civics. Our teacher Mrs. Levy got us interested in the 1976 presidential campaign by making half the class Democrats for Jimmy Carter and the other half Republicans for Gerald Ford, and scheduling a series of debates and rallies. I fell into the Carter camp and enthusiastically threw myself into the battle, ardently following his stump speeches on television, drawing posters, and even visiting the local Democratic campaign office for buttons and bumper stickers to share with my team. My attempts to convince my parents of his obvious superior qualifications met with eye rolls. Like most Lubavitchers, they leaned somewhat toward the right politically and were still angry about what had happened to Nixon, who had been a friend to Israel. When Carter won, I felt smugly triumphant, as though I'd personally swept him into victory.

I was diligent if not always enthusiastic about most of my religious classes. I plodded through the priestly rituals in Leviticus—the minutiae of ablutions and vestments, the endless offerings of bulls, goats, and lambs, lightened only occasionally by a juicy section on forbidden sexual relationships or nocturnal emissions, or macabre guidelines for stoning sinners or handling lepers. *Pirkei Avot,* the collection of Mishnaic teachings on ethics, seemed simplistic and irrelevant; it would be many years before I could appreciate the subtle wisdom of maxims such as "Obtain for yourself a teacher, acquire for yourself a friend, and judge each person favorably." Still, I loved picking through Rashi's commentaries on the Bible, decoding the cryptic acronyms in his strange Hebrew script as though solving a puzzle. And I never tired of the biblical stories, many of which satisfied my adolescent thirst for Sturm und Drang. My heart broke at Isaac's innocent question, "But Father, where is the sheep for the offering?" as Abraham leads him up Mount Moriah, at Jacob's grief when he's shown Joseph's bloodstained coat, at Moses's silent resignation when God shows him the Promised Land that he will not enter with the Children of Israel. The romance of Ruth the Moabite and Boaz was to die for. Gleaning the fallen sheaves in his field with the other poor people, she catches the eye of her kinsman.

> At mealtime, Boaz said to her, "Come over here and partake of the meal and dip your morsel in the vinegar." So she sat down beside the reapers. And he handed her roasted grain, she ate her fill and had some left over.

I did not consider myself particularly religious, at least not in any meaningfully spiritual sense, the way my parents were. The idea of an all-powerful, all-knowing God provided no sense of comfort. Deep philosophical questions, such as how we could have free will if God knew everything, or how He allows terrible things to happen in the world, simply weren't interesting to me. I preferred dealing with facts on the ground—an observant Jew who was in it solely for the clarity and regularity of the rituals. Tzip and I still went to shul every week; the Lubavitchers had finally moved from Orchard Street to a new *shtiebl* close to home. I enjoyed *davening* with the others, but I never prayed on my own and rarely contemplated the meaning of the words I recited. What appealed was the formality of the service and the satisfaction of mastering the directives—when to sit and when to stand, where to answer Amen, what to say quietly, and when to simply listen as the hazan prayed aloud. The call-and-response of *Kedushah,* the whispered paragraphs of *Shemoneh Esreyh* were unambiguous, almost meditative, a connection more to the people praying around me than to God.

I do not know what force led me there, but as soon as the stack of *Ms.* magazines disappeared from the dressing alcove of my parents' bedroom, I headed straight for my mother's bed and inched my fingers between box spring and mattress until I hit something solid. I yanked out two magazines, took them to my room, and continued the education my mother had interrupted when she'd found me reading them the day before.

"Hmm. Those aren't really for you," she had said.

"Oh? How come?" I asked.

"Maybe when you're older," she replied as she took them away. I stomped off in a huff.

I knew perfectly well what she meant, of course. Many other

magazines came to the house—*Good Housekeeping, Ladies' Home Journal, Time, National Geographic,* even *Vogue* occasionally—but *Ms.* was clearly of a different order. It was feminist, but in a very different way than Marlo Thomas's cheerfully liberated recording of "Free to Be . . . You and Me," which seemed to be playing on everyone's turntables in the 1970s. I had been initially drawn to *Ms.* by a cover photo of a woman's bruised face. Feeling slightly queasy, I flipped through issue after issue to read about wire hanger abortions, domestic abuse, the Equal Rights Amendment, the housewife's "moment of truth," and stewardesses who got fired for being too fat. Perhaps most shocking to me was the fact that they were speaking—or, more accurately, raging, demanding, screaming—about these things at all. It was the opposite of *tznius,* of what I had been taught I was supposed to be: a modest, God-fearing, self-effacing woman who lived a home-centered life. It was even more troubling and more riveting than the *Playboy* magazine I'd peeked at in the drugstore. What I read in those issues of *Ms.* touched me deeply. I wondered whether my father had seen them.

"Maybe when you're older," my mother said firmly.

She had not actually purchased the magazines herself but had borrowed them from a daring friend going through a "rebellious" phase. To all appearances, my mother was decidedly not going through a rebellious phase. She was pregnant with my youngest sister, Suri, and would soon be busy with a new baby. More to the point, she possessed a natural *eydelkeit,* a sweetly refined sensibility, the flip side of which was an almost pathological fear of saying or doing anything that might cause others to criticize her. And yet, a pile of *Ms.* magazines somehow made its way into our home, as did Nora Ephron's *Crazy Salad,* which my mother did, in fact, buy and which I parsed so thoroughly that I could have quoted long passages from memory, had anyone asked. That book, too, was a revelation, filled with hilarious ruminations on such unmentionable subjects as the shackles of ladylike behavior and the problem with feminine hygiene sprays. My hormones were surging, my body transforming itself into something I could barely recognize, and in five years I might be married and on my way to motherhood. I was terrified, but I learned from Ephron and from Gloria Steinem that you could joke about embarrassing things, and maybe even protest or stomp your feet about them, and that was okay. To me, these women were slivers of light shining through a door that had been opened just a crack. I couldn't even imagine what was on the other side, but I was beginning to think that it was where I'd find myself someday.

But in the meantime, there was eighth-grade graduation to get through. We proceeded down the aisle in our blue caps and gowns, and sat alongside the stage in our designated seats, girls in the front, boys in the back. Our principal, Rabbi Hirschman, took the podium and asked everyone to rise as he read the Rebbe's letter of congratulations, which reminded us of the privilege of a Torah education and exhorted us to lead good Hasidic lives. Rabbi Hirschman then launched into his own speech, and I found my attention wandering over to the audience—parents, kids, and teachers as familiar to me as the layout of my house. It was all so comfortable, but comfortable was the last thing I was looking for. I wanted different and a little scary—the thrill of walking down a new high school hallway, anxiously scanning the faces of strangers who might someday become friends. I wanted to write for a school newspaper and join some sort of "club." I wanted to take Latin and wear a lettered sweater. Instead, the next four years promised to be just like the last eight, only with fewer girls and no boys. From far away, I heard Rabbi Hirschman's speech building to a crescendo, followed by polite applause. Then he began calling us one by one to the stage, and as I made my way up the stairs I'd climbed a hundred times before, a sob burst out of my chest. When Rabbi Hirschman presented me with my diploma in its vinyl case and a copy of *My Prayer,* a book of commentary on the siddur that each of us received as a gift, he mistook my misery for bittersweet nostalgia and smiled at me benevolently. I could tell what he was thinking: *Chaya Deitsch, another job well done.*

That Saturday night, Jess, one of my more sophisticated classmates, threw a graduation party; the following September she would be starting public school. It was our first—and last—mixed boy-girl party and my mother had been reluctant to let me go, but she finally gave in. Sure enough, several hours in, with the radio blasting "Love to Love You, Baby," Jess dimmed the lights in her basement rec room and with a mischievous smile announced that it was time for Spin the Bottle. I froze, waiting to see what my friends would do. None of us had ever kissed a boy, but Jess would brook no objections. Jordana's cheeks turned bright pink as she trudged toward the circle, followed reluctantly by Ariella and then Tzip. I stepped in to join them, when I felt someone tap my arm. It was Seth.

"Hey, can I talk to you?" he asked. "Alone?"

He led me down the hall to Jess's bedroom and closed the door. We stood there face-to-face and I began to tremble. The air grew exceedingly warm. Was I going to faint?

"Don't look so nervous," Seth said, rather nervously. Maybe he'd be the one to faint, I thought.

I tried to think of a witty response, but my brain had shut down and my throat was so tight that even if something had come to me, no sound could have passed through it.

Seth took my hot hand in his own sweaty paw. "I'm sure you know that I've liked you for a while now."

This was news to me. *I like you, too,* I wanted to say, but the best I could do was nod gratefully.

"Can't you say something?" he asked.

"Thanks," I croaked.

Words came out of Seth's mouth but I couldn't take them in. After ten months of ploys and daydreams, I was completely unprepared for success. Why wasn't this fun? If it had been a movie, we would have collapsed into each other's arms and, with no words necessary, shared our first, magical kiss. Instead, we just stood there, awkwardly looking at each other, while I tried to figure out how to extricate my hand from his moist grip.

"I guess my timing isn't great, since I'm leaving for camp in the morning," he said, a little sheepishly. And in the fall, he said, he would be dorming at a boys' yeshiva in Riverdale, New York. "Maybe we can write each other, though."

I lunged for a pen on Jess's desk and managed to recover my voice. "Sure," I gasped. He scribbled on a piece of paper, and that was that. When Seth and I rejoined the party, Ariella greeted me with a raised eyebrow. I just shook my head. Nope. Not this time, anyway.

Just me and the girls for the next four years. Maybe that wasn't such a bad idea after all.

7

Canary in the Mineshaft

My uncle set my small suitcase on the landing and handed me my garment bag.

"You're sure they're home?" he asked. I nodded. I could hear voices in the house.

"Okay then. We'll pick you up after Yom Tov. Send regards."

"Thanks a lot." I waved again to my aunt and cousins waiting in the car, and rang the bell.

I was in Crown Heights for Simchas Torah. Over the past few years I'd been making regular visits to my Gurewitz relatives for Shabbos and the Jewish holidays and now, at age fourteen, I felt very grown-up visiting them on my own. It was nice to have Bubby and Zaydie fuss over me, serving me cookies and coffee as I attempted, with whatever scraps of Yiddish I could muster, to tell them about school and send them love from my mother. I'd also cultivated my own small group of Crown Heights friends, girls I'd met in camp and at the bungalow colony where we spent summers, and we'd pass the time on Shabbos afternoons walking around the neighborhood or lounging in someone's bedroom.

But mostly I came to spend time with my cousin Shayna. We'd grown closer than ever since I'd started high school and become a "mensch," as she joked. Shayna had graduated high school the year before and was working toward a teacher's certificate at the Bais Rivkah seminary. Our time together felt precious. Shayna was just weeks away from her eighteenth birthday; she would almost certainly be married within a year or two, and then off into a whole different world.

"Chaya Slave!" Uncle Zalman exclaimed as he opened the door and greeted me with his usual riff on my middle name, Slava. He kissed me on the cheek and apologized for not taking my bag. "You aunt has forbidden me to lug anything." He looked tired, still recovering from bypass surgery the year before.

I found Shayna upstairs in her room, expertly placing a hank of hair around a hot roller. In her lacy champagne-colored slip, she looked sensuous, like Elizabeth Taylor in *Cat on a Hot Tin Roof.* I suddenly felt like a lumberjack.

"I should get curlers like those," I said.

"Please, you don't need them. You have such great hair. Mine is horrible. Let's see what you're wearing."

I hung my garment bag in her closet and unzipped it reluctantly. Next to Shayna's silky wardrobe, my own Loehmann's specials, which I'd loved an hour ago, looked practically dowdy. I displayed a red floral print dress with slimming pleats down the center front and back.

"I love it," she said. "Maybe I'll borrow it." I snorted. She'd swim in it.

As the sky darkened we quickly finished dressing, lit the candles that ushered in the holiday, and then made our way to 770. The mid-October air was chilly, but when we opened the door to the packed women's section of the shul on Eastern Parkway we were hit with a blast of humid heat from the press of bodies inside.

As a little kid, I'd loved Simchas Torah, riding on my father's shoulders at the Orchard Street Shul as we marched behind the men carrying the velvet-covered Torah scrolls for hours past my bedtime. I'd be handed a paper flag to wave, as well as steady infusions of cake and soda to keep me awake. The holiday became less interesting as I grew older, turning instead into a test of how long I could stand to watch the men dance with the Torahs up front while I stood with the other girls in the back. The scene in Crown Heights was even less fun if you were a female past the age of seven. Enhancing the celebration of the holiday with a few shots of vodka was a common practice for the men, but by the end of the second day of the two-day holiday, drunken men could be seen weaving along the streets arm in arm, vomiting into hedges or out of windows. A few could be observed chasing after women and trying to kiss them.

The drinking would not begin in earnest until the next day, but I knew the services that night would continue well past midnight. Shayna and I planned to spend just an hour or two watching the men dancing downstairs and then go home to eat with my aunt. But assessing the mass of women inside, I hesitated. Shayna grabbed my hand and pulled me in.

"Follow me," she ordered, ramming through the crowd like an icebreaker. My New England reserve feebly asserted itself. "Forget it, Shayna. I don't need to go up close."

She ignored me. "Out-of-towner coming through!" she barked. "She needs to see."

Within minutes, we'd made it close to the front. Through the Plexiglas, I scanned the men's section below. It was even more crowded down there, and the hot air literally steamed with the intensity of the dancing. I searched for the Rebbe in his usual corner but couldn't spot him.

We had been there about an hour when the tenor of the noise downstairs suddenly shifted. Singing turned to loud murmuring and then into shouts. As the women surged forward to see what had happened, a panicked young man ran into the women's gallery. "Get out of my way!" he screamed, pushing the ladies and children aside as he moved toward the front. He grabbed a chair and swung at the plastic until it cracked and a large jagged chunk tumbled into the men's section. He kept at it until he'd made a hole about four feet across, sending cold outside air flowing into the stickiness below.

I clutched Shayna's hand once again as the crowd sucked us into the courtyard. Amid the pandemonium, we began piecing together what had happened. The Rebbe had collapsed, and Hatzolah, the local Jewish private ambulance service, had taken him away in the ambulance that was always parked in front of 770. I looked around. Everyone seemed stunned, myself included. Some were crying, others reciting psalms to pray for his recovery. It was strangely quiet, as though we were underwater. I pictured the Rebbe grimacing, his knees buckling, and trying to catch himself on his prayer stand before collapsing. I knew he was human, of course, but even as he'd grown grayer and stouter over the years, I'd never thought of his having a body like everyone else, with organs that could fail. When as a child I dreamed of him disappearing, it was just that—he'd simply be gone. It never occurred to me that he might die. As I looked at the grieving, terrified people around me, I rapidly cycled through a series of emotions: sadness that the Rebbe was unwell and sympathy for all his apparently traumatized followers, then relief at this evidence that he was mortal just like the rest of us, and then, of course, guilt at my callousness, and fear that even just thinking these thoughts would get me into trouble. For the rest of the holiday people talked of nothing but the Rebbe's condition, trading rumors and bits of information that trickled in from the hardy few who'd made the walk to and from Mount Sinai Hospital, in Manhattan, where he'd been admitted for a massive heart attack. He would be okay, people reassured one another; his medical care was the best of the best.

Back in New Haven, I enjoyed a brief celebrity as an eyewitness to the event. The Rebbe's recovery over the next few weeks somehow became even further proof of his invincibility. I kept my opinions to myself.

I was one of seven ninth-grade students in our school. This made us the largest class of the Beth Chana-Hannah Academy High School for Girls, as well as the only class. The high school had been in existence since the early 1960s—one of my aunts had been in the first graduating class—but over the years it would periodically close from a dearth of enrollment. Not wanting to send us away to New York, our parents persuaded Rabbi Hirschman to air out the unused classrooms and hire a few high school–level teachers. His first acquisition was Andrew H. R. St. George III, a tweedy WASP in his mid-fifties who served as both principal for secular studies and our English teacher. Mr. St. George radiated a gracious charm and easy manner that made him as exotic to us as we were to him. We'd heard that he had come to us from a longstanding teaching stint at Andover in Massachusetts, which left us wondering why he'd taken this job, for what must have been a vast reduction in salary and professional standing. He took a laid-back approach to education, spending most of our freshman English classes reading aloud short stories, usually something humorous by James Thurber or Mark Twain.

Mr. St. George used his Ivy League connections to hire additional faculty, seeking out impoverished Yale graduate students willing to trek out to the suburbs for the teaching experience and for a salary, however meager, that was certainly more than they'd be making as tutors or au pairs. Among his finds were a strikingly handsome math instructor from the Yale Divinity School and a French teacher whose husband was finishing his PhD. When our parents requested extracurricular activities, he tapped the Yale School of Drama for someone who could teach us a bit about acting and work with us to produce school plays. And so one afternoon we were introduced to a very tall, very thin woman in her mid-twenties with glossy red hair, high cheekbones, and smooth skin with a disturbingly gray pallor. She wore a green velvet cutaway blazer, a yellow prairie skirt, round glasses, and brown lace-up boots. When she smiled at us, her two front teeth protruded slightly. I couldn't tell if she was artsy or just crazy.

"Hi, girls! I'm Annabel Edwards."

We stared. She grew briefly flustered and then clapped her hands. I noticed her graceful, tapered fingers.

"Okay. Up you go! Now form a circle in the middle of the room. Start walking around, only . . ."

She paused, thinking, and then chuckled.

". . . the room is filled with grape Jell-O."

Soon we were all strenuously wading through Jell-O, our arms pushing at an unseen mass. Embarrassed giggles gave way to intense concentration. When Annabel finally let us return to our seats, I felt charged, exhilarated. And with that, the girls of Beth Chana-Hannah Academy embarked on an unexpected education in the latest techniques of modern and experimental theater. Every week, we'd begin with a warm-up improvisation.

"Tzip, Jordana, Karen! Three toddlers trying to reach a toy off a high shelf." They dropped to their knees at once, grabbing at nothing above.

"Chaya, come here." As my friends cooed and babbled, Annabel whispered in my ear. "Okay, you're an escaped convict, but you can't say so. Make them figure it out." I nodded and hobbled toward the group, one leg dragging an imaginary ball and chain.

After improvisation exercises, Annabel would pull a stack of mimeographed sheets from her battered leather bag and have us read aloud scenes from playwrights we'd never heard of: Pirandello, Ionesco, Genet, Beckett. I was smitten, not by the acting, which I quickly and with no regrets realized I had little talent for, but by the very language of the plays. Absurdist dramas such as Ionesco's *The Bald Soprano* struck me as miraculously profound, a live wire making contact with my teenage angst.

Mrs. Martin: When you looked in the mirror this morning, you didn't see yourself.
Mr. Martin: That's because I wasn't there yet.

My mind was officially blown.

We staged our first production in early April—Jean Giradoux's *The Madwoman of Chaillot*. Dispensing with the fourth wall, Annabel turned the chairs around and had us perform at the back of the auditorium instead of the stage. On cue, I stepped into my scene, threw open my arms, and promptly forgot my lines. When the (figurative) curtain finally fell, we received rousing ovations from the dedicated cluster of teachers and slightly puzzled relatives who'd come to see us.

That spring a tragicomedy of a different sort was playing out at the home of Aunt Yocheved and Uncle Zalman in Crown Heights: the real-life drama of marrying off their daughter Shayna, at age eighteen and a half on schedule to become a wife and mother. Finding an appropriate spouse for one's child was customarily carried out with discretion, a few phone calls made to well-connected Lubavitchers who might know of someone who had a son or a daughter of the right age, temperament, economic prospects, and religious level. Ideally, the bull's-eye would be hit with the first attempt, or perhaps the second, and after a few dates—typically, sodas in a Manhattan hotel lobby—the engagement would be announced. My uncle, only half-jokingly, offered a case of Jack Daniel's to whichever matchmaker succeeded in finding a husband for Shayna. Aunt Yocheved drew my mother into nightly phone discussions, reviewing and rejecting the list of candidates.

"Someone said Chezkie ran around when he was younger. They heard he had a motorcycle."

"Yankel has a brilliant mind, the top student at yeshiva, but Shayna needs someone in business. A rebbetzin's life is not for her."

"People say Mendel's a nice guy, but, *ach,* his older sister is not all there in the head."

I eavesdropped on these conversations with great interest.

Shayna was my canary in the mineshaft of adulthood. Here was a sneak preview of the ordeal I would be expected to undergo four or, at the latest, five years from now. I avoided the topic with my mother but, in a gesture of what she probably perceived as supreme open-mindedness, she said to me one day, "You know, I think that eighteen might be a little young."

"Oh, good," I said, considerably relieved.

She nodded. "Nineteen seems just right to me."

Nineteen did not seem right to me at all. I wondered how far I could push things before the community whispering would begin. Twenty-four sounded appealing, but that was way too late, I knew. Most of the good boys would have been snagged by then. Twenty-one, I decided, would give me a few independent years past high school, and my family's credentials—rabbinic lineage on the Gurewitz side and a successful family business on the Deitsch side—would ensure that a three-year delay would not significantly diminish the stream of eligible young men available for my consideration. For a guy with no formal secular education or professional direction, marrying me would be hitting the nuptial jackpot, as it came with the expectation of receiving either a managerial position at my grandfather's factory or some capital to start his own business.

Not knowing any Lubavitcher boys my age other than cousins, I wondered whom my parents would turn up. When my mother asked me what kind of man I dreamed of marrying, I drew a blank. "Smart, I guess," I lamely replied. It seemed like the wrong time to admit that what I really wanted was someone from outside the Lubavitcher community—someone either less religious or not religious at all. And I knew that there would never be a good time to share with my mother the heretical thought that getting married was not really a priority with me in the first place.

In the meantime, the search for Shayna's *bashert*, her destined life partner, was taking longer than expected. The dutiful daughter surprised and distressed her parents by turning down one suggestion after another. When I came to visit, she complained about the men her parents had chosen.

"These guys, all they want to talk about is themselves. They just don't seem serious about anything."

I tried to sympathize with her disappointment but selfishly wanted to keep her single for as long as possible. Perhaps, like me, she secretly didn't want to get married.

Finally, that winter, she struck gold. I overheard conversations about a guy in Chicago named Levi, from a nice family. Over the course of a month, Shayna went out with him five or six times—he flew to New York for their dates—and after a brief moment of panicked indecision, Shayna consented to the match. My uncle phoned in the particulars to the Rebbe's secretary, who conferred the Rebbe's approval several hours later. It was only then that it was officially "official."

I had not spoken to Shayna throughout her accelerated courtship. This was new territory for us. That night, I finally called her to wish her mazel tov and to give her the third degree.

"So, what's he like?" I asked.

"I dunno," she said, laughing. "He's a nice guy. You'll meet him and see."

"Is he handsome?"

"Yeah, I think so, anyway. He's thin, with curly brown hair and a short beard. He trims it." She sounded very happy.

"When do you think the wedding'll be?"

"Sometime in late May, we're thinking, right after Shavuos."
Four months away.

"Will you live in Chicago?"

"We'll have to. That's where the family business is—appliances."
She paused. "Lotsa snow."

"No kidding."

And, just like that, the Shayna I knew was gone.

Over the next few months, as Shayna prepared for both her wedding and the move to Chicago, she tried to make me part of the tumult. She introduced me to Levi, calling me her "younger sister, only better." He was as nice as promised and said they were setting up a special guest room for me in their new apartment. She displayed the armloads of clothes and shoes she'd bought, as well as the dishes and towels and silver candlesticks she needed to set up house. I managed to muster up some excitement (I had to admit her new wardrobe was to die for), but mostly I felt left behind and jealous of her happiness. I longed for the familial and communal approval Shayna had so magically acquired, but domesticity was a domain I found about as tantalizing as the polyurethane my father obsessed over in his factory.

The day of the wedding, my family and I arrived at Aunt Yocheved and Uncle Zalman's house a few hours early to get into our finery. I was quite pleased with my gown, a blue silk chiffon with butterfly sleeves, purchased at Remin's, a fancy dress shop in Westchester. The original low-cut neckline had been expertly filled in by a seamstress, who had taken the fabric from the bottom of the dress; one of the advantages to being short was the ease with which clothing could be made *tznius*-appropriate. I finished off the outfit with strappy white sandals, three-inch stiletto heels I could barely walk in. When we were done, my mother and I found Shayna upstairs in her room, her hair in rollers. Her wedding dress hung on the door frame of her closet, its satin skirt so pouffed with crinolines and tissue paper, it could practically stand on its own. Tense as I'd ever seen her, she seemed to be channeling every ounce of concentration into holding back tears that would smear her makeup. She'd been fasting all day, as was Levi, and would not eat until after the ceremony. The two hadn't seen each other all week, although they'd spoken on the phone many times a day.

Shayna took the rollers out of her hair, gently fingered the curls into soft waves around her face, and, for the last time ever, sprayed it all into place. Aunt Yocheved and my mother helped her pin the veil into her hair, the three of them debating how far back on her head it should sit. At last, Shayna stepped into her dress and the transformation was complete. I had to admit, she looked truly beautiful, ethereal. As I watched her cross the threshold of her childhood room and make her way downstairs, I bade her a silent, sad farewell.

The ceremony took place out of doors, in front of 770. I watched as Levi slipped the plain gold wedding band onto Shayna's index finger, uttering the words that would bind them together as husband and wife:

Ha'ray aht mikudeshes lee bitaba'as zu, kidas Moshe v'Yisroel.
Behold you are sanctified to me, according to the laws of
    Moses and Israel.

Then he stomped on the glass that had been rolled up in a napkin (a reminder, in the midst of celebration, of the Holy Temple that had been destroyed by the Romans in Jerusalem in 70 CE), and everyone erupted in deafeningly euphoric mazel tovs. Shayna and Levi made their way through the crowd like the celebrities they were that night, with friends and relatives pulling at them in congratulations. As they went past me, I managed to reach out and touch Shayna's hand. She turned, and when she saw it was me, her eyes lit up. I leaned in to give her a hug.

"Mazel tov, Shayna! Wow!" I was sincerely delighted for her.

"I know!" she replied. "I can't believe it!" She squeezed my hand and disappeared into the vortex of well-wishers. My feet throbbed. No longer able to walk unassisted on my three-inch heels, I looked around for my father to prop me up.

As we headed back to the catering hall, I steeled myself for the barrage of *you're next!*s that would be hurled my way throughout the night like dozens of bridal bouquets.

"Mazel tov, Chaya! God willing, by you, too!"

"We should hear good news from you soon, Chaya!"

"You look so grown-up! How old are you?"

Each time, I would smile brightly and agree enthusiastically. And silently repeat to myself, over and over, *I am never doing this. Ever.*

8

Valley Girl

Tenth grade came to a close with our class production of *The Importance of Being Earnest*. Unlike the tangled plot lines of *The Madwoman of Chaillot* that we'd butchered the year before, Oscar Wilde's satire on the tightly circumscribed social milieu of Victorian England suited us very well. I played Cecily, the sheltered ward of Jack Worthing, a sober country squire leading a double life in London. Tzip played Algernon Moncrieff, Jack's friend and a food-obsessed esthete who falls in love with Cecily. My costume was a snug, floral, yellow, low-cut number, borrowed from Annabel, who was blissfully unaware of the rules of modesty for Hasidic girls. The dress was beyond un-*tznius,* and I looked great in it. The second act opens with Cecily alone in the garden, tending a hedge of roses. Leaning forward with my watering can, I recognized my mother's gasp from the audience as my newly amplified bosom presented itself to family and friends. The evening was a triumph.

I was widening my cultural sphere in other ways as well. Nearly every Sunday, I took the bus downtown, heading first to Atticus Bookstore, where I read my way through the fiction shelves. Sometimes I sat at one of their small café tables with my new purchase, nursing a cup of coffee. On my way home, I stopped in at Cutler's Records and Tapes, where I had undertaken an accelerated education in popular music. Flipping through album after album, I studied the cover art and liner notes as rigorously as one of my history texts. I usually left with a record or a piece of sheet music. Back home, I would subject my family to endless pounding on the living-room piano—Billy Joel's "Only the Good Die Young" and "Point of Know Return," a whiny ballad by Kansas. I sang along, badly, touched by lyrics that felt as though they were written just for me. *"Sooner or later it comes down to fate. . . ."* My taste in music eventually advanced from the Bee Gees and the soundtrack from *Grease* to more serious rock: the Beatles, the Cars, Queen, Styx, ELO, and my ultimate favorites, the Rolling Stones. Shut up in my room, I alternated between listening to WPLR, New Haven's top rock station, and creating my own mix tapes. My stereo, a Chanukah present from my parents, took pride of place next to my bed.

As with my reading matter, my parents tolerated these secular musical journeys surprisingly well. My mother had loved the Everly Brothers as a girl, and would croon lyrics from "Wake Up Little Suzy" at the stove; many nights we had fallen asleep to her renditions of "Chantilly Lace" and "Yellow Polkadot Bikini." To my parents, Mick Jagger was simply an updated Elvis, a harmless diversion. My father would oblige me with the necessary ten or fifteen dollars to feed my music habit, and my mother even drove Jordana and me to an Andy Gibb concert at the New Haven Coliseum. As she let us off at the curb, we heard the sound of glass shattering in the distance. My mother shook her head, muttered, "I must be crazy to let you do this," and drove off.

They responded less benignly to other rebellions, however, drawing sharp battle lines over clothing. The men's V-neck Hanes T-shirts that I paired with sweeping Indian print skirts, jangly earrings, and blue beaded moccasins were a particular bone of contention. The problem was that the sleeves barely grazed the top of my biceps, leaving exposed a huge, forbidden swath of upper arm and elbow. I loved these shirts, because they highlighted what I considered the two best features of my chunky adolescent figure: the above-mentioned cleavage, albeit less exposed than Cecily's, and my thin arms. Unlike hard-rock records and contemporary novels, which were more discreet forms of adolescent rebellion, clothing was a public declaration of where you stood on the observance scale. Short sleeves placed me firmly on the "trampy" end. While I more or less adhered to the school's *tznius* code on weekdays, weekends were my time for self-expression. As I would go downstairs on Sunday mornings, I would brace myself for pursed lips, a raised eyebrow, and, eventually, an argument. The probability of victory hovered at somewhere near fifty percent, but I believed I had begun to wear my mother down.

"Put on a sweater. You are not leaving the house like that."

"What's the big deal? It's three inches. Anyway, it's just New Haven."

"As I have told you many times before, Chaya, reputation matters in our world. People are looking at you, and they're going to judge you. You'll be known as a girl who wears short sleeves and that puts you in a certain category. It will limit your chances."

"What do I care?"

"Sweater. Now."

"I'll put one in my bag."

My father recused himself from all discussions involving fashion, choosing to focus instead on my increasing truancy from shul on Shabbos mornings. Tzip still stopped by every week to pick me up, but now, more often than not, I'd beg off and send her on her way alone. If I showed up at all, it was late, just as services were wrapping up. I wasn't technically required to pray at all, I argued, pointing out that my mother never *davened,* except for the four or five times a year she went to shul for the major holidays. Still, I had been my father's most enthusiastic shul-going companion, and he was disappointed. More and more often he came home to find me reading on the couch with my sisters. "Where were you?" he'd ask crossly, and I'd shrug.

Shabbos in general had become for me a catchall of grievances and bad feeling. My resentment had little to do with restrictions on my activities; most of my friends were Sabbath observant. Rather, Shabbos was weekly salt poured on the wound of broader restraints placed on me as a female consigned to the back of the shul and to scullery duty at Friday night dinner and Saturday lunch. As my mother, my sisters, and I—and whichever other women had joined us—scurried to clear plates and fetch the next course, my father and the male guests remained in their seats from the time the challah was sliced until Grace After Meals. They seemed almost cemented there by some testosterone-and-tradition-laced substance. And when the spirit moved them, the *niggunim* would begin: loud, table-pounding, wordless melodies in which women were forbidden to participate and which drowned out any conversation we could have among ourselves. We were, in effect, muzzled until they were done. It drove me crazy. I was tired of being silenced.

That said, I was still a good Lubavitcher daughter. The few transgressions I'd allowed myself were strictly small potatoes: ripping open an interesting-looking envelope on Shabbos, eating candy bars that lacked a kashrus seal, muttering during morning prayers instead of mouthing the actual words. Major vices felt too irreversible, too beyond the pale even to contemplate. Pork, shrimp, lobster—the trifecta of hard-core nonkosher—I barely even considered them food. I'd as soon take a bite of my desk chair as touch a McDonald's French fry, which Rabbi Hirschman swore was cooked in horse fat. Despite my anger at mealtimes, the proscriptions of Shabbos remained sacrosanct; even in private I didn't write or turn the lights on or off. And boys, while certainly of interest, were as elusive as yeti in the all-female environment I inhabited. But even as no unclean thing had passed my lips, my inner life felt *trayf* in the extreme, a cauldron of forbidden yearnings that mashed together the dairy of secular intellectual exploration with the meat of physical longing. Straining against generations of custom and obedience was a tug toward freedom—roiling, wanton, inexpressible. In my lonely shame and confusion, these desires felt more disgraceful than the most heinous sin I could cobble together: eating a ham-and-cheese sandwich on Yom Kippur, naked, in front of the Rebbe's picture.

During the day I kept my adolescent demons in check, but they would come up for air once darkness fell. The pattern was always the same. I'd fall asleep at eleven, after prime-time television, and would suddenly awaken two hours later, springing bolt upright in bed, my heart racing. Wide-eyed with fear, I would search out the by-now-familiar shadows—an ominous two-inch stump under the closet door, the rhombus on the wall in the hallway. Terrified and groggy, I waited for the shapes to move and reveal the escaped convict who had made his way into the house to kill us all, prevented from carrying out his plan only by my wakeful vigilance. I would stay locked in the same position for hours, too paralyzed to relieve the torture by flicking on a lamp, picking up a book, or playing my beloved radio. At first light the phantoms would suddenly vanish, allowing me to fall back into a deep sleep for an hour or so. On the worst nights, I'd gather my blanket and pillow, scurry to my parents' bedroom, and camp out on the floor, slinking back to my room in the morning. If my parents noticed these nocturnal visits, they didn't mention them.

Although I'd more or less stopped having birthday parties after my bas mitzvah, my sixteenth birthday seemed to need commemorating. An official sweet-sixteen party felt tantalizingly secular to me, a milestone that would put me in step with the rest of American teenage culture. Absent male attendees, however, my coming-out party didn't really go anywhere. My mother baked my favorite cake, chocolate with peanut-butter icing, and the usual group of girlfriends came over to hang out in my room, a last hurrah before most of us dispersed for the summer. We spent the next few hours as we always did, gossiping, listening to music, and eventually hopping up for an energetic round of *Saturday Night Fever* line dancing, which had somehow managed to make its way even into the women's sections of Lubavitcher weddings, where even matronly Hasidic ladies tried their darnedest to look like John Travolta on the dance floor. Then we trooped downstairs to the dining room to join the rest of the party: my sisters, hungrily eyeing the cake and soda on the table; my grandmother and the local aunts, drinking coffee; and my mother's friend Nadia, who gave me a flat rectangular package wrapped in purple, with a knowing look.

When seen side by side, Nadia and my mother made for unlikely companions. My mother was petite, refined, and cautious, never without lipstick and always in dark colors, trying to camouflage a surplus twenty pounds. Nadia was tall, flamboyant, and patchouli scented, a former flower child and poet who had become a Lubavitcher only a few years earlier, when she'd met her future husband. Nadia had for the most part submitted to her new role as *frum* housewife, but she did so under protest, and the one concession she refused to make was covering the long auburn waves that hung down her back.

Beneath the surface, however, the two women had much in common, sharing a sly sense of humor, a love of ideas and culture, and highly sensitized radar for the foibles of human nature. Their kitchen table conversations ranged from novels to paintings to irritation with so-and-so to mothers-in-law and back again to novels. For Nadia, my mother served as a sympathetic guide to the often bewildering mores of the community she had joined. And in Nadia, my mother found a loyal confidante and a safe channel to secular culture, someone who could relate both to the beauty of a Diebenkorn canvas and irritation with a husband who had once again overimbibed with his cronies at the kiddush in shul after *davening*. Nadia took a pointed interest in my development into adulthood. Recognizing my restlessness, she told me stories from her student days at Berkeley, introduced me to Milan Kundera and poetry by Stevie Smith. She would listen to me practice piano and exclaim over the genius of my clunky, ad hoc interpretations of a Scarlatti sonatina. It was from her that I first learned the term "Felliniesque," and that lobster tastes nothing like chicken. At shul one Shabbos, she pulled aside the curtain separating the women from the men and gestured toward a cluster of young boys vigorously swaying and chanting. "Can you imagine *marrying* one of them?" she stage-whispered. I blushed and shook my head. "No way."

Now, as I peeled back the wrapping of her birthday gift, she scanned my face for a reaction.

"Your mother will probably kill me," she said, "but I think you'll really get it. Her show just opened in San Francisco."

It was the exhibition catalog for Judy Chicago's *The Dinner Party,* the art installation that was the subject of a great deal of media attention in 1979 (which I had missed entirely). I thumbed through the pages to demonstrate my appreciation, noting photos of richly glazed ceramic plates, colorful undulations of wings and hollows; I wondered if they really were what I thought they were. Alone in my room that night, I studied the book more closely. Titillated at first by the profusion of vaginas—the lacy labia on Emily Dickinson's plate, the color of strawberry yogurt, were particularly disturbing—I was soon captivated by the text, brief biographies of women I'd never heard of: Boadicea, Hildegard of Bingen, Sacajawea, Sojourner Truth. Each one, it seemed, had burst onto the historical record by defying the expectations of her time and society: the Celtic warrior queen facing down the Romans; the brilliant abbess, theologian, and medical woman; the Shoshone guide steering Lewis and Clark through the unknown West; the bold former slave and abolitionist.

What soil had nurtured their courage? Seeking clues, I filtered their experiences through the lens of my own circumstances. Would my father ever encourage me to attend law school as Anna van Schurman's had, even if it meant sitting behind a curtain during class? Would I, Margaret Sanger–like, be driven by ideological passion, or would outraged intelligence propel me to action, as it had Mary Wollstonecraft? Compared with the achievements of these women, my own dreams seemed at once petty and unattainable: discussing Nietzsche during impassioned late-night debates with college friends, living in Manhattan on my own dime, kissing a boy I had no plans to marry, pulling on a pair of Levi's. And yet, as inconsequential as these experiences were, it felt as though my very life depended on seeing them through.

I considered my own female lineage. How had Bubby Gurewitz managed on her own with her husband in the gulag? What gave my great-grandmother, Hinda Deitsch, the courage to travel a thousand miles from her home to get her son released from a Soviet labor camp? What had made my dignified Bubby Deitsch so fearless? As a young woman in Kharkov, literally one day before the Nazis entered the city, she had pushed her way through a mob to buy train tickets to Tashkent for her family's escape. I tried to picture a twenty-five-year-old me shoving through panicked crowds, shouting down a Soviet ticket booth clerk. It was impossible. I was still too shy to buy sanitary napkins at the local pharmacy.

"But how did you *do* it, Bubby?" My question seemed to surprise her.

"What do you mean, how? I just did it. You would do it, too."

I wasn't so sure about that. Had Bubby known why I was asking, I would have gotten an earful. I just hoped that when the time came for me to go my own way, I had half the grit of the women who had preceded me.

A week after the party, I found myself in the American Airlines terminal at JFK with seven other Lubavitcher girls. We were headed to Los Angeles for the summer to work as counselors in

Camp Gan Israel. The day camp, run by the local Chabad House, was one of five or six that had sprouted across Los Angeles County. The mandate from the *shluchim,* the Chabad emissaries who had hired us, was unequivocal: in between the usual fun activities, we were to do all we could to make *yiddishkeit,* observant Judaism, appealing to the unaffiliated Jewish kids in our care.

I was lucky to get the job. Although the Gan Israel franchise ran day camps across the country, a counselor job in Southern California was the summer employment Holy Grail. The location offered constant sunshine as well as the promise of unending after-hours diversion: the glitz of Beverly Hills and Hollywood Boulevard, movie star sightings, our pick of kosher restaurants. My companions and I were to be in charge of the girls and the smallest children; a group of teenage Lubavitcher boys, booked on a separate flight, would ride herd on the boys' section.

The *shluchim* had carefully screened the list of applicants to weed out the "bums," who might see a summer away from home as an opportunity to sow wild oats. The ideal candidate would be lively but serious, devout but not so otherworldly that she would scare off the unobservant campers. In addition to phone interviews, applicants' names had been run past Crown Heights high school principals. As an out-of-town Lubavitcher, I skated in mostly via connections. The *shluchim* for our camp, Leibel and Simi, knew my family from way back; more crucially, Simi and my aunt Miri, herself a *shli'ach* in L.A., were close friends. My cousin Rochel, who'd already been accepted, sealed the deal by vouching for me.

As I moved through airport security, I ignored the anxiety rising in my chest. I looked no different from anyone in that chattering cluster of girls—most of us in long-sleeved T-shirts, pantyhose, and long denim skirts with the back slit sewn up—but I knew I'd gotten in under false pretenses. Not only were my religious beliefs shaky—not least my loyalty to the Rebbe and his urgent calls for the Messiah—but my feelings for the children of strangers ran a very short gamut from indifference to irritation. I wondered how long I could keep up the charade. Still, I had not wanted to spend the summer in New Haven, and my parents had urged me to go. My aunt assured me that I could spend every Shabbos with her and her family.

During the flight, Rochel walked me through the aisles to introduce me to our fellow counselors. At sixteen, I was the baby of the group. Come September, the rest—seventeen- and eighteen-year-olds—would be seniors in high school, in their first year of seminary, or engaged. I was also one of only three girls not from Crown Heights and the only one who didn't attend the Crown Heights girls' high school. We touched down at LAX after dark and were met by our aptly named head counselor, Chani Briskman. A tall, wiry nineteen-year-old, she looked as though she'd been born with a clipboard in her hand. We loaded ourselves into the slightly dinged blue van that was to be our transport for the summer, and as we sped north on Interstate 405, Chani delivered some unwelcome news.

"There's been a slight adjustment in our living situation. Our rental won't be ready for another week or so. Until then, we'll be camping out at the Chabad House."

We'd been set up in the library, a wide room ringed on three sides by floor-to-ceiling bookshelves. A long plastic accordion partition, as sound- and lightproof as paper, stretched across a doorway in the fourth wall. Tables and dozens of chairs had been stacked and pushed against the other walls to make space for two rows of bare cots. After a late dinner and a brief meeting with Leibel and Simi, we made up our beds, slipped into our nightgowns or oversized sleeping T-shirts, and, in two straight lines worthy of Madeline and her roommates, settled down for the night. Long after midnight, someone finally turned out the lights and I lay there in the dark, surrounded by books of psalms, prayer books, oversized volumes of Talmud, and a very large painting of the Rebbe, roughly the same size as the one we had at home. Nine weeks and counting, I thought.

The next morning, I surveyed the grounds. The Chabad House was a sprawling ranch-style building along a busy street in Tarzana. Converted from a private residence, the public rooms served as shul, dining hall, classrooms, and rabbi's office. Out back stood a second, smaller house where Leibel and Simi lived with their young children. They were in their early thirties but seemed older, with the gravitas that comes from being spiritual mentors. And indeed, their nonstop outreach—free Shabbos meals, Hasidic philosophy classes, Hebrew after-school programs, Passover seders, Purim parties, and summer camp—had paid off. Their relatively new Chabad House had become one of the largest in the San Fernando Valley, with a following of dozens of Jewish families and singles. Regardless of their levels of observance, all were gathered into Leibel and Simi's uncritical embrace, warmed by their ardent belief in their mission of bringing Jews back to God.

While living at the Chabad House, I encountered a continual flow of people who had shrugged off their old lives to seek meaning in practices and beliefs that had been abandoned by their parents and grandparents long before they were born. Back home, I'd known only a few *ba'alei teshuvah,* "returnees" to the faith, like my mother's friend Nadia. I was baffled by these people, who were enthusiastically taking on what I was so eager to throw off.

Watching these newcomers master unfamiliar customs was like watching adults learn to walk after a stroke: the intense concentration as they awkwardly performed the ritual hand-washing before eating bread, as they self-consciously touched the mezuzah nailed to the doorpost and then brought their fingers to their lips for a quick kiss, as they fervently replied *baruch Hashem,* thank God, to a simple how-are-you. Rituals that were second nature to me looked strange and unfamiliar in their inexpert hands. "Have you met the Rebbe?" a woman asked me one day. We had been talking about New York. "No, not really," I said and, seeing her face fall, added limply, "but I've seen him from a distance." I found her earnestness—and my insincerity—depressing. Beyond small talk, we had no common ground. What kind of person, I wondered, would voluntarily assume the privations of a Lubavitcher life, would deliberately leap into a box and pull the lid up over her head? How could I connect with this woman? I coveted the carte blanche of her old life, even as she longed to shoulder the baggage I was trying so hard to discard.

Camp began two days later, with lineup next to the entrance of Lake Balboa Park. The boys' section was gathering a discreet distance away. I looked over at their counselors, who were frantically trying to assemble their charges into something approximating rows. Calculating my chances for a summer crush, I surveyed the array of embryonic beards, buzz cuts, plate-size yarmulkes, and woolen tzitzis dangling from beneath Gan Israel T-shirts. No one tantalized.

I was in charge of the youngest group, a cluster of five-year-old

Jessicas, Jasons, Kristins, and Kimberlys, open-faced and tawny-skinned. My junior counselor, an eighth-grader with white blond hair named Denise, wore tiny terry-cloth shorts that showed off her coltish legs and displayed a Valley Girl attitude that bounced from sulking to sarcasm to eye-rolling boredom. We were just three years apart, but in my long skirt, patterned knee-highs, and Gan Israel shirt layered on top of a three-quarter-sleeved T-shirt, I looked and felt like a middle-aged rebbetzin—as provincial to her as the male counselors seemed to me. I was meant to be a good influence on Denise, but I couldn't see that happening. I was clearly the last thing she wanted to emulate.

Chani called the camp to order. "Good morning, everyone, and welcome to Camp Gan Israel! We're going to have a great summer together. Before I tell you about our activities, we need to thank God for letting us get up today and enjoy one another's company. Here's a thank-you song that we'll sing every morning!"

At our briefing the day before, Chani had reminded us to be alert to our ultimate goal. "These kids know *nothing*," she had said, shaking her head at the tragedy. "Not Shabbos, not kosher, not nothing. So you're going to have to start from scratch with them."

Now I walked up and down my row of small charges, brightly enunciating the Hebrew syllables. My mind, on the other hand, floated somewhere else, to escape the humiliation of being part of this spectacle and the guilt I felt at my hypocrisy.

"Mo-deh ah-nee li-fa-neh-cha. . . ."

Puzzled stares from the children and Denise. We would have to practice during rest period.

That first week sped by in a blur of swimming, arts and crafts, relay races, snacks, and pre-Shabbos parties. At the end of each day, I sank into the Chabad House couch, exhausted from hunting down wet towels and stray socks, chasing errant campers across playgrounds, and, always, yelling myself hoarse to make them sing louder.

Hashem is here *(point to chest)*
Hashem is there *(point away from chest)*
Hashem is truly everywhere *(raise both arms and make a wide, sweeping arc)*
Up, up, down, down, right, left, and all around *(more pointing and sweeping)*
Here, there, and everywhere *(still more pointing and a big, dramatic sweeping finale)*
That's where He can be found.

We counselors finally moved into our own place, another California ranch house on a busy thoroughfare. It had been hastily and sparsely furnished—bunk beds for the four bedrooms, a few worn sofas and a long folding table in the living room. A pristine pool table, racked and ready, also took up some space in the living room, no doubt left behind by the home's owner.

The kitchen was stocked with pots, pans, cutlery, and dishes, and we were given a generous allowance to buy groceries. Once a week someone from the Chabad House delivered fresh cases of glatt kosher meat and *Cholov Yisroel* milk. Chavi, ever the organizer, hung a cooking-and-cleanup assignment grid on the refrigerator door.

With no television but a van and gas card at our disposal, our nights were given over to explorations of Los Angeles. One of the girls with a driver's license would take the wheel, tearing up and around the hairpin turns of Laurel Canyon and Mulholland Drive. Once in the city, we might travel west to Venice Beach to check out the street performers, or east to Hollywood Boulevard, where we gawked at prostitutes and took turns trying to fit our feet into Gloria Swanson's tiny cement impressions in front of Grauman's Chinese Theatre. Creeping along Sunset Boulevard, movie-star map in hand, we gawked at the mansions of long-dead silver-screen idols.

Even as we took in the sights, we attracted no small amount of attention ourselves. As a gang of spirited teenage girls, we naturally generated a din, but it was our appearance—the neck-to-calf coverage, the stockings on sticky summer nights—that made heads turn. People thought we were Amish. One night on the Santa Monica pier, two guys approached and tried to flirt. Safely away from the Crown Heights microscope, a few of the bolder counselors got into the spirit of it. I just watched, nervous but fascinated by their daring.

"Hey, where you girls from?"

"New York. Now can I ask *you* a question?"

"You bet."

"Why do wear your sunglasses at night?"

"'Cause I like the way it looks. What's your name?"

"Gitty. And this is Miriam."

"Pretty. I'm Justin. Nice to meet you." As he thrust out his hand, I held my breath. The game was up.

"I'm sorry, but we're not allowed to shake men's hands," Gitty said politely. "Our religion forbids it."

Justin awkwardly withdrew his hand. He looked embarrassed.

"I was just being friendly," he said, a bit defensively. He and his friend quickly walked away.

On Wednesdays we stayed on our side of the mountain and joined the choked traffic on Van Nuys Boulevard for the Valley's famous cruise night. We inched our battered vehicle through the parade of souped-up muscle cars and meticulously restored classics as Led Zeppelin and Pink Floyd blared into the street. We felt as though we had been dropped onto another planet. As usual, for some of the girls the opportunity to interact with the locals was irresistible.

"Look at that idiot's car! His seat is practically on the floor!"

"I know! I'm going to say something."

"No, don't!"

"Pardon me, sir . . . Yes, you. What kind of car is that? . . . From Brooklyn . . . My eyes? That's very kind of you . . . No, we don't date."

As we drove away, the other counselors were doubled over with laughter, thrilled by their friend's audacity and incredulous at this latest example of *goyishe* stupidity. Bolstered by an enviable mix of naïveté and moral certitude, the girls confidently dismissed anything that deviated from their norm, from the world of Torah and the pronouncements of the Rebbe, as *shtuss,* vain nonsense. The idea that non-Jews could be thoughtful or smart or content with their lives was irrelevant, even outside the realm of possibility. But the world they mocked was the world I aspired to, and I couldn't join in the merriment, even at a spectacle as bizarre as cruise night. Their contempt felt personal. It hit me with full force that summer that if I were ever to leave religious life, there would be consequences. I would be deliberately unlinking myself from the community, and I would become an object of pity and gossip. I wondered if I would miss the unquestioned acceptance I enjoyed in the Lubavitcher world. Would my relatives turn their backs when they saw me? I allowed a tiny, terrifying thought to emerge—What if my parents sent me away?—before crushing it into blackness.

Aunt Miri was one relative I didn't think I would ever have to worry about. As promised, she had beds waiting for my cousin Rochel and me every Shabbos. I adored her as much as ever. She took naturally to Southern California, mashing together devotion to the Rebbe with the L.A. fascination with lifestyle gurus: nutritionists and psychic home decorators and color experts who divined by determining your "season" not only what clothes you should wear but also your personality type. "You're a classic winter," Miri told me, watching me arrange my toiletries on the dresser top. "No question about it."

Like all *shluchim,* my aunt and uncle would host a table full of guests on Friday nights. Shabbos mornings, however, were Miri's time to reclaim herself. She'd send her three young children off to shul, fix herself a mug of coffee, and stretch out on the couch with a stack of library books. Lying on the rug with my own reading material, I would listen to her describe, in her Gurewitz soprano, the bargains she'd snagged that week at I. Magnin, or tell stories about some of the odder congregants at my uncle's shul. Three time zones away, I knew my mother would be doing the very same thing in New Haven; spending time with Aunt Miri felt almost like being at home. These Shabbos visits kept me going as the weeks of camp went slogging by.

The mother of all Chabad Houses was in Westwood, at the edge of the UCLA campus. A converted office building, it was the first

Chabad outreach center for college students to be set up in America, by an emissary of the Rebbe, in 1969. It was also the largest, with a sizable full-time staff—from the rabbis who prowled the campus looking for, as they joked, "any Jew that moves" to the administrators, fund-raisers, and cooks who kept the place going. Nearly ten years after opening its first doors in California, the Chabad House had become a well-known destination for students on campuses throughout the United States who were looking for Shabbos services, meals, social events, and intense debates on Hasidic philosophy. Both the conversations and the hospitality seemed to resonate with young people who were searching for meaning, or perhaps simply lonely or homesick.

In mid-August, our group of counselors was invited to the Westwood Chabad House to celebrate Shabbos Nachamu, the first weekend after the Tisha B'Av fast day, which had been the culmination of a three-week period of mourning for the destruction of the Holy Temple in Jerusalem nearly two thousand years ago. We arrived on a hot Friday afternoon shortly before Shabbos candle lighting and were directed upstairs to a wing of dormitory-style bedrooms, where we unpacked, did our makeup, and got into nice dresses and heels. Back downstairs we joined a mixed crowd of Lubavitchers and university students waiting for dinner to be served; the latter were casually dressed, though all of the women knew to wear skirts and not pants. Before the kiddush was recited, we were introduced as "honored guests from Crown Heights." As was the case at the Chabad House in Tarzana, I found myself being intensively studied by the students for signs of Rebbe aura.

Keeping up the pretense for this large an audience was more than I could handle. I stayed silent during the meal and fought the urge to push my chair back and flee to my room. Instead of engaging the students in conversations about the joys of Hasidism, I passed the time in a series of daydreams that ranged from meeting Mick Jagger on Hollywood Boulevard to buying a cute jersey I'd seen in a boutique window. These pleasant distractions helped me tune out the impassioned homily delivered by one of the *shluchim* and then, inevitably, the deafening rounds of *niggunim*. A few of the male students had by this point mastered not only the complex melodies but also the rapt pose that marked a true Hasid caught up in the fervor of sacred song: fist pounding the table, upper body swaying back and forth, eyes squeezed shut. I felt like I was back at our Shabbos table at home, with all of the accompanying feelings of resentment.

Shabbos morning was even more oppressively hot than the night before. After creeping down to the kitchen for a cup of coffee and a cheese Danish, I skipped shul and spent the morning reading in bed. At noon, Rochel came to fetch me for lunch. The crowd was smaller this time, with some new faces. Waiting for the challah to be cut, I noticed a student sitting at the other end of the table. He looked about twenty, attractive but not too handsome, clean shaven, with brown hair that he wore shorter than many of the long-haired Chabad House habitués. He had clearly arrived bareheaded; perched on his head was one of those hideous satin yarmulkes from the bin near the door. A newbie. I caught his glance on several occasions during lunch, hastily looking away each time, until he finally smiled at me. I felt myself blushing, a tendency that I hated, and mentally staged the first act of our great romance. When the meal ended, he disappeared in the crush of people getting up from the table, and although I loitered in the common room for a half hour pretending to examine a rack of brochures, he never materialized.

We had a long afternoon ahead of us. Between my lazy morning and stillborn crush I was feeling restless, so when a few of the girls proposed a stroll across the UCLA campus I was happy to join them. We crossed through the main gate on Le Conte and stepped into a scene of idyllic college life. The campus was summer-Saturday quiet, but here and there we spotted groups of students in shorts and T-shirts laughing in the shade of a tree or tossing around a Frisbee. A shirt-sleeved man carrying a bundle of files, obviously a professor, cut across the quad and headed into one of the massive Romanesque buildings. A group of runners pounded past us, training for their fall meets. Having grown up in New Haven, I was not unfamiliar with a university campus, but where Yale's Gothic structures intermingled with downtown shops and traffic, UCLA was completely shielded from the business of everyday life. The expanse of pure and unadulterated academia made my heart ache with longing.

Later that day, as we relaxed in the common room waiting for Shabbos to end, my mystery man reappeared. He was walking down the hallway toward the shul for the evening prayer service and happened to glance in my direction. Once again I blushed, hardly believing my good fortune. I was determined not to let this second opportunity slip through my fingers and spent the next half hour with an ear cocked toward the shul, listening for the *davening* to end. As soon as it did I sprang from the couch, ignoring my cousin's raised eyebrows at my sudden eagerness to participate in the havdalah ceremony that marked the end of Shabbos.

There were only about twenty men in the shul, many fewer

than the night before. One of the rabbis filled his kiddush cup, while someone else lit the havdalah candle and held it high so everyone could see. I spotted my friend and nonchalantly made my way toward him. He looked at me and smiled. I noticed that he had blue eyes.

"Hi," he said. "I'm Eric." He didn't try to shake my hand. Obviously not that much of a newbie.

"I'm Chaya. I'm with the Tarzana counselors."

"I know. I saw you before."

The ceremony began and we lowered our voices to a whisper. At the first blessing, the *bisomim* packet of cloves and cinnamon that was being handed around was passed to me and I held it to my nose, inhaling the sweet fragrance. As I passed it to Eric, I felt a jolt at the pressure of his fingers on the paper. A moment later we raised our hands toward the flame of the havdalah candle so that the light was reflected onto our nails—a mystical reminder that before Adam and Eve ate from the Tree of Knowledge, our bodies were clothed in nothing but pure light. After the ceremony, as everyone else was enthusiastically wishing one another— depending on their level of proficiency—a good week, a *gut voch,* or a *shavua tov,* Eric and I migrated back to the hallway and found ourselves outside, on the front terrace. Leaning against the balustrade, standing close but not touching, we quickly began swapping stories. Eric was studying environmental science, a discipline I'd never heard of. He'd been coming to the Chabad House for about four months now and loved the atmosphere. Mildly disappointed, I told him about my favorite novels and TV shows, made jokes about the kids at camp, even teased him about his beanie yarmulke. I needed him to understand that I wasn't like the other counselors. The banter was exhilarating. Watching him laugh, I felt as though I'd assumed a new identity. I was a girl whom cool boys liked.

"Hey, are you coming to the party tonight?" Eric asked. The Chabad House was hosting a Shabbos Nachamu party. Inwardly I groaned, envisioning guitars, separate circles of dancing for men and women, and platters of fruit and marble cake. Still, I would have endured almost anything for a little more time with Eric. But I couldn't figure out a way to pull it off.

"I don't think so," I replied. "We have to get back to the Valley." The counselors were planning a drive through Bel-Air and dinner at the kosher pizza shop, and there was no way I could stay behind unchaperoned. Just by going off on my own in the Chabad House and talking with Eric, I'd already ventured into forbidden territory. This was most definitely not what we counselors had been brought to Westwood for. Many of the *shluchim* had seen us talking, and I knew Aunt Miri would hear about it before the night was out. I didn't care in the least, but I knew that was going to be it for Eric and me.

"Too bad. It's been really great talking to you."

"Same here. Good luck with your environmental science."

Later that night in the van, on the way to Bel-Air, one of the girls turned to me with a glint in her eye.

"So, Chaya, you seemed to have passed a pleasant Shabbos."

I gave her what I hoped was an enigmatic smile.

"Yes," I said, "it was most interesting." It was, in fact, more than just interesting. It was a tantalizing glimpse into an unknowable future.

9

My Messiah Arrives

"Jesus! You've got good blood! I know you wouldn't shoot a lady!"
Mr. St. George's refined tenor tightened into an urgent southern
falsetto weighed down by regret and fear. We were nearing the end
of "A Good Man Is Hard to Find," Flannery O'Connor's comi-
cally creepy gothic story, and the meddlesome grandmother is
pleading with the Misfit to spare her life. I shuddered, not sure if
I wanted her to live or die.

These small frissons aside, however, I was bored and unhappy.
Junior year was shaping up to be much like sophomore year. Our
class had dwindled to six girls, but my sister Ricki and four fellow freshmen added another grade to our tiny high school. That
gave Annabel eleven actors for her experimental staging of Bertolt
Brecht's *The Caucasian Chalk Circle,* which would be performed
in the round. She reassured us that despite a cast list of fifty-plus,
we could easily compensate for the shortage of actors by taking on
multiple roles and wearing signs bearing the characters' names—
peasant woman, limping man, girl tractorist, wealthy kulak, and
so on—which we could switch as needed. The potential for offense
in presenting the work of a Communist playwright glorifying col-
lectivized agriculture to an audience of survivors of Stalin's Russia
was apparently lost on Annabel. Fortunately, with long blocks of

the script crossed out for what she called "manageability," there was no danger of anyone in the audience following the story.

There was also a belated attempt by Rabbi Hirschman to infuse some Hasidism into our religious education, with the hiring of Mrs. Goldschmidt, a Lubavitcher who had just moved to New Haven with her new husband. Young and deeply devout, she rhapsodized about the soul's yearning for divine light in a charming Italian accent, having grown up in Milan. She was small and thin, wore no makeup, and her wardrobe consisted for the most part of beige and brown A-line skirts paired with neat collared shirts buttoned all the way up to the neck. Her short brunette *sheitel* was strictly utilitarian. She was not unattractive, yet she managed to squelch any emanations of sensuality. Later in the year, when she could no longer hide the growing bump in her middle, her face turned pink if she caught us glancing at it.

Mrs. Goldschmidt was a true believer, viewing the world through the lens of the Rebbe's teachings and through the *Tanya,* the complex central text of Chabad philosophy and theology written by Rabbi Shneur Zalman of Liadi, the founder of Lubavitch Hasidism. My own understanding of these subjects was superficial at best. I knew that Chabad was an acronym for the Hebrew words *chochmah, binah,* and *da'as*—wisdom, understanding, and knowledge, the three pillars of human intellect—and that they topped a complex hierarchy of *sefiros,* or mystical levels of proximity to God. I had heard of the *sitra achra* and *klipah,* both of which had something to do with kabbalistic ideas of impurity. But I didn't know enough about any of this to connect these concepts to anything in my personal life, and I certainly couldn't look to the *Tanya* as most Lubavitchers did, as a guide to spiritual self-improvement. Although my father studied a portion of the *Tanya* every day, I'd never been motivated to even peek into one of the two or three copies that he kept at home. Mrs. Goldschmidt's teachings didn't succeed in making it any more accessible or interesting to me.

But she was nothing if not determined to improve our spiritual lives. In her efforts to purge our environment of taint from the outside world, Mrs. Goldschmidt locked horns with Mr. St. George in a polite daily struggle over a framed *Romeo and Juliet* movie poster that had hung in the high school library ever since anyone could remember. It wasn't that Mrs. Goldschmidt found Shakespeare offensive, but the photo of Leonard Whiting and Olivia Hussey in an amorous embrace had to go. Every morning she unhooked the poster from the wall and slid it behind an armchair near the door. After she'd gone for the day, Mr. St. George would retrieve it and rehang it, without comment. This went on for weeks, until eventually Mr. St. George gently pulled rank and the lovers remained on view.

She also tried to up the *tznius* level of the students. I suppose she sought my support as a fellow Lubavitcher, but instead she brought out the worst in me.

"A girl's beauty is inside," she told me, stabbing a finger at her chest. She looked mournfully at my crimson scoop-necked blouse. "Red draws attention to the wrong things."

I'd had these bromides about inner beauty spooned into me since I was a child; I didn't buy it at age ten and now it made me furious. The more Mrs. Goldschmidt scolded, the more pointedly I tried to show her up. My sexy red shirt became my personal Shakespeare poster. I wore it as often as laundry would allow. She never lost her temper with me, but neither did she tire of trying to persuade me to see the error of my ways. I had to admit that part of me envied the tranquility and certitude that her faith gave her. I, in turn, felt like a hungry baby rooting for something to latch on to. Religion is meant to add structure and a sense of purpose, even joy, to one's life, but I felt trapped by it. Custom and ritual did little to nourish me or lead me deeper into belief.

My friends should have given me sustenance, but they weren't enough. We were a tight bunch of nice, smart girls who were beloved by our teachers, hung around together on Shabbos afternoons, went to the movies together, and signed up en masse for jazz dance and swimming lessons at the downtown YWCA. Most of us had known one another since nursery school.

I loved my friends, but when I was with them I felt like I was choking on pudding. And I could never seem to shake an inner feeling of loneliness, no matter how many people I was with. Interaction required effort, with diminishing returns. By day I presented myself as outgoing, opinionated, funny, confident, and adventurous, only to come home drained and craving solitude. My classmates spent hours on the phone with one another, but I had no words for what I felt and wanted. And even if I had, the stakes were different for me than they were for the other girls. Tzip, also a Lubavitcher, seemed less restless and rebellious, and found strength in the anchor of community; she had no reason not to toe the line. The other girls, second- and third-generation Modern Orthodox American Jews, didn't live under the same tight press of expectations or struggle with the guilt of shedding Hasidic traditions that had been preserved through war, prison, disease, hunger, and displacement. They, too, would likely follow in their parents' footsteps. I, on the other hand, was traveling solo into new territory, confused and full of dread.

Absent like-minded companions in the flesh, I turned to writers who might be my fellow travelers. Günter Grass, Dylan Thomas, Albert Camus, Kurt Vonnegut, Muriel Spark, J. D. Salinger—anyone who dealt in agita and disorientation, with protagonists who had been metaphorically blindfolded, spun around, and delivered back to a world gone awry was right for me. And, just for fun, I read *The Godfather* at least twice and kept an illicit copy of Judith Krantz's *Scruples* at the back of my bookshelf. I would lose myself in old movies, settling into the well of my vinyl beanbag chair (a sample from my father's factory), watching two or three in a row on the small black-and-white set my parents had won in a raffle and given to me.

If I kept it together in front of my friends, my family bore the brunt of my discontent. I had less and less patience for my sisters—I was a drill sergeant over clearing the supper table and a resentful martyr if they didn't listen. Battles with my parents intensified, not just over clothes but ideology as well. I railed at my father that the Torah needed to change with the times, heresy to someone with his deep and unshakable faith. An uncommunicative man to begin with, his responses to my outrage ranged from confusion to panic, a beleaguered shopkeeper waiting out a deranged customer.

"But Dad, why can't women participate in shul, actually be part of the *davening* up front?"

"So come to shul more often."

"You know that's not what I'm talking about."

"Please." He'd sigh. "Don't be like that."

But I *was* like that, and I didn't know how—or even want—to be any different.

My mother was only slightly more sympathetic. She viewed her own foray into feminism as conceptual rather than aspirational. From her vantage point, I'd been given an exceptional degree of cultural and even religious freedom, but I was taking it too far, rebelling simply for the sake of rebelling. When I challenged her by saying that maybe just being a good person was enough, and that following all those religious requirements and prohibitions wasn't necessary for living a moral life, she was furious. "You and your humanism!" she spat out. "There *is* such a thing as the Torah!"

But I could see that, surface irritation aside, my parents were deeply concerned about me and my restlessness, which only made me even angrier. Once-rational conversations inevitably devolved into tears and door slamming.

Back in my room, with Heart's "Magic Man" blaring mournfully in the background, I indulged in melodramatic fantasies in which I'd die or slip into a coma. Prostrate with grief and remorse, my parents would cling to my inert body,

Too soon to lose my baby
Yet my girl should be at home.

One night, well after eleven, I decided I'd had enough. I was going to run away, somewhere. I pulled a sweater on over my nightgown, got into my sneakers, and stomped downstairs. I opened the front door and slammed it behind me, hoping to God it was loud enough to wake my parents. Shivering from the cold concrete, I sat on the front steps and sobbed. After a few minutes, I heard the door open behind me.

"Chaya?" It was my mother, wearing a robe and hastily tying a kerchief over her hair. "What are you doing out here?" Her voice was high-pitched, worried. My father was right behind her.

"Leave me alone!" I shrieked. "You don't care about me. You don't want me to be happy." My voice rang out, amplified by the silence of the empty street.

"What are you talking about?" my father said. "Come inside. Now." He sounded frustrated but his voice barely registered. I felt like I was drowning and didn't know whether I wanted to be rescued or allowed to disappear. I jumped up and started running down the sidewalk.

"Hey!" my father yelled.

I stopped and whirled around to face them. "Leave me alone!" I shrieked again. "You just need me for babysitting. You just care about the other kids." Even as I hurled the accusation, I knew that wasn't the real problem, but it was the first thing I could think of.

"That's not true!" my mother protested. "Don't you know we love you the most?" (Many years later, I learned that at one time or another, my mother had said this to each of us.) "Please come inside." She put her arm around my shoulders and led me back in. We were both crying.

When I came down to breakfast the next day, I acted as though nothing had happened, but I could feel my mother's eyes on me as I made my coffee and dumped cereal into a bowl.

"How are you?"

"Better."

"Yes?"

"Yes."

"Good."

Did she really believe me? I had no idea, and I was too exhausted to ask her.

That spring, my classmates and I began taking college entrance exams. Although we were attending a Lubavitcher yeshiva, the school acknowledged that most of their non-Lubavitcher students would go on to college. I'd not yet floated the idea to my parents, fearing a definitive veto, but I went through the process with everyone else, as though attending university was a foregone conclusion. As it turned out, my parents had no objection to my taking the exams. I'd always scored high on standardized tests and they were pleased when I did well in school. In truth, I was as ignorant as they were about the college admissions process, let alone what life would be like once I arrived on campus. Over the years, we'd had a number of Modern Orthodox Yale students join us for Shabbos meals, but to my mind these observant Ivy League Jews belonged to a rarefied club, separate from the rest of humanity. I assumed I would be allowed to attend Stern College, Yeshiva University's school for women, in midtown Manhattan. Although I longed for what I perceived as a real campus experience—complete with men and non-Jews and quads and no curfews—Stern would be better than nothing.

And, besides, I loved New York. Aside from class trips to the Statue of Liberty and the American Museum of Natural History, my personal experience with the city had been largely confined to Brooklyn. Still, I believed I'd come to know Manhattan through books and television: *The Catcher in the Rye, That Girl, Satur-day Night Live, Kojak.* I took my first unchaperoned train trip there in eighth grade, when a classmate treated three of us to the Ice Capades in Madison Square Garden for her birthday. More recently, family trips to the city had become a regular occurrence, thanks to a new business connection of my father's who gave us tickets to first-run Broadway shows, courtesy of his corporate entertainment account. We would come into the city for Sunday matinees—*Annie, Peter Pan,* and, a high point, the new production of *Sweeney Todd* with Angela Lansbury and Len Cariou—and we usually capped the day with dinner at Moshe Peking, a kosher Chinese restaurant near the theater district, feasting on blazing pu pu platters and glazed spareribs. Each time the office towers of midtown Manhattan came into view from the car window, I was dazzled anew by the grit and the noise, and I jealously eyed the people going about their business with a blasé sophistication that contrasted sharply with the openmouthed wonder of day-trippers like us. I couldn't wait to be one of them.

Mr. St. George gave his notice in late spring and finally solved the mystery of his presence at Beth Chana by revealing to us his struggle with alcoholism, the condition that had ended his career at Andover. He had been able to get his problem under control, and it was now time for him to move on. His lassitude as a teacher aside, we were all sorry to see him leave, parents included. Emi-nently respectful of Jewish customs and a gracious speaker at grad-uations and other school events, he'd smoothed our rough yeshiva edges.

The same could not be said of his replacement, hired shortly before the school year ended. Gentility was a trait Dorothy Wolfe neither practiced nor admired. Train wreck, tornado, steamroller, force of nature—whatever metaphor one chose, she was determined to deliver culture and enlightenment to a tragically misguided bunch of girls benumbed by what she deemed religious superstition. How she bamboozled her way past Rabbi Hirschman and into the job was yet another mystery.

Dottie, as she insisted we call her, looked to be somewhere in her early forties, with frizzy red hair she tried to corral into a tightly pinned bun. She told us that she was divorced and that she had a young son. She had an easy smile and the same bulging-eye condition as Marty Feldman, which lent her an expression of perpetual attention and warm surprise. Required to conform to the Orthodox dress code, she'd assembled a hodgepodge of matronly knit suits and vintage dresses that showed off a curvy figure. She spoke fluent Russian and French, and just enough Yiddish to make it clear that while she knew what we were about, she herself had deliberately chosen a more cosmopolitan, intellectual path.

Dottie was not simply assimilated, she was a true *apikoris,* proudly Jewish and just as proudly antireligious. I'd never met this type of person in the flesh, but I had been trained from childhood to both loathe and fear the scoffer, the heretic, the dreaded Jewish secular intellectual who turned tradition on its head. I was fascinated by her. She embodied the difference between the jazzy klezmer music showcased in Greenwich Village clubs and the kvetchy accordion arrangements I danced to at weddings and bar mitzvahs. She was a cultural and intellectual descendant of the notorious *Yiddishistn,* the pre-Bolshevik movement that lured young Jewish men and women out of the shtetl and into modern, secular Russian life, while keeping cultural ties to the old ways for artistic inspiration.

For Hasidim, the *Yiddishistn* were worse than the tsars. Both at home and at school the works of writers such as I. L. Peretz and Mendele Mocher Sforim occupied the same shelf of banned books as *Mein Kampf* and *Das Kapital*. (*Fiddler on the Roof*, based on Sholem Aleichem's Tevye stories, was the exception, not just tolerated but beloved, and made acceptable perhaps by Tevye's refusal to accept his daughter's marriage to a Russian gentile. I saw it at the Shubert Theater in New Haven when I was five, cowering in my mother's lap when Fruma Sarah rose from the grave.) These secular Yiddish writers, although rarely Communists themselves, were seen by the Hasidim as precursors to the hated Bolsheviks to whom they also lost children, first ideologically and then physically, as many eventually vanished into the gulags. Virtually every Lubavitcher family could claim a relative who'd tragically crossed over to the other side. In mine, a great-aunt and great-uncle on my father's side stayed behind in the Soviet Union when everyone left. On my mother's side I had a great-great uncle who was literally and derisively known as Aryeh der Apikoris; he was the purportedly brilliant apostate brother of my revered and learned great-grandfather, Reb Itche der Masmid. So when one of their numbers, in the person of Dottie Wolfe, actually took the reins of our education, the Orthodox parents, and mine especially, went on high alert.

It took Dottie exactly no time to sniff me out. She had taken over Mr. St. George's English class and was horrified to discover that we had never learned to write a proper essay. Gone was story hour, replaced by spirited discussions of *Inferno, The Return of the Native,* and the Romantic poets. She had us read *Macbeth* aloud in class, so that we could hear the music of Shakespeare's language. Protesting at first, I soon felt energized and excited as we dug deeply into literary analysis of these works. Dottie flattered me with private jokes and gossip about the headmaster and the other teachers. I felt clever around her and craved her admiration. One day, when she gave us a pop quiz and I asked for a "piece" of paper—rather than a "sheet," as she'd instructed us to say—she tore off a tiny corner and handed it to me with a smirk. "Will there be more than one question?" I asked, not missing a beat, and was rewarded with a guffaw that puffed my chest with pride. I struggled mightily over my first real essay, on Virgil's role as Dante's guide, staring at the blank lined paper waiting for something to come. Wads of rejects piled up around my chair as I crafted and recrafted my opening paragraph, thesaurus in my lap, building up my argument so painstakingly that I burst into tears every half hour or so just to relieve the pressure. Two days later I finally managed to fill five pages with tiny script, my knuckles so cramped I could barely release my pen. Dottie hated it. Aside from a few reluctant check marks, the paper was a snarl of red, with a disappointed "I know you can do better" scrawled across the top. I was devastated but she made me to do it over, following the comments she'd made in the margins. It was no easier the second time, but the finished product was, in fact, much improved.

By the time we broke for the summer, something in me had, at last, changed.

10

Off the Cliff

With no plans for the next two months, I returned to the Valley for another day camp stint, ultimately a poor decision. It was hard for me even to pretend to be interested in introducing little kids to religious observance. My cousin Rochel, head counselor that summer, was too sweet to give me a hard time about my obvious neglect of my duties, even when some of the parents complained. I counted the days until I could leave.

When we returned to school that fall there was a new girl in our senior class. Lisa was a recent *ba'alas teshuvah* from upstate who lived a highly idiosyncratic version of religious life. She had persuaded her wealthy, bewildered parents to build a separate kosher kitchen for her in their guesthouse, which she shared with her boyfriend, Matt, a pot-smoking musician in his early twenties who drove up from Brooklyn each week to spend Shabbos with her. Even more exotic, she had self-confidence to spare, embracing her no-longer-fashionable hippie esthetic as the height of chic. And although the hem of her denim skirt brushed demurely against her ankles as she swayed and murmured during morning prayers, she freely shared with us the details of her sex life and swore like a sailor. "Go fuck my dog, Rabbi," she once whispered behind a teacher's back when he said something that met with her disapproval, and then kissed her upraised middle finger for emphasis.

I was in equal measure repelled and fascinated by her. Lisa seemed unburdened by any sense of consequences, willing to try anything. I would have been glad for a sliver of her attitude, just enough to dampen the alarms of conscience that made me feel guilty even when I was being good. I weighed my words as though they were grains of plutonium. No thought or idea was allowed to advance without first being run through a fine filter, tested for parental disappointment and community opprobrium. Lisa, at least on the surface, didn't seem to care what the rest of the world thought about anything she did or said. I, on the other hand, cared way too much.

I felt most sure of myself when I was literally in the driver's seat, having gotten my license in the summer, before I left for California. My mother drove a Pontiac LeMans, which we nicknamed LeMon for the time it spent at the shop, and my father, a wood-paneled Buick station wagon. I was happy to take either, inwardly marveling at my competence in backing out of the driveway, steering into a parking spot, merging onto highway traffic, working the windshield wipers, and accelerating at just the right point of the curve. My mother put me on supermarket detail, and I was also regularly tasked with picking up and dropping off my sisters, duties I assumed without complaint as they allowed me to get behind the wheel. Punching the button that I had preset to WPLR, I force-fed my captives a steady stream of Donna Summer, the Knack, Gloria Gaynor, the Doobie Brothers, and Queen. Before long, even the younger kids were joining in on "Bohemian Rhapsody."

My reward for doing errands was use of the car to shuttle my friends around. On Saturday and Sunday nights we'd head for the multiplex in Milford or take in something arty at the York Square

Cinema downtown. Afterward, we'd drive along quiet residential streets, complaining about our teachers or talking about clothes. If it was early enough, we might stop at Friendly's for sundaes.

It was my idea to turn the car into a smoking lounge. Cigarettes were not officially forbidden to Lubavitcher women, but those who did smoke, especially in the open, were considered unrefined, even sexually aggressive. My father had smoked cigars for a time, a habit he shared with his father, but never in the house, as the smell made my mother queasy; he'd quit altogether several years earlier. I had been practicing for a while at home in front of my bedroom mirror with unsharpened pencils, channeling scenes from old movies. Thus far I'd mastered two poses: languorously sexy, like Lauren Bacall in *The Big Sleep,* and in-your-face rebellious, like Paul Newman in *Cool Hand Luke,* complete with exhalation of smoke right into the warden's face. I felt ready for the real thing and convinced my friends to join me.

We bought our first pack of cigarettes after a long debate in the Walgreens parking lot over which brand to choose. Winston and Marlboro were too macho, we agreed, unfiltered Camel and Lucky Strike too harsh. We narrowed it down to Salem and Virginia Slims before settling on the latter because of the feminist message in its ads: "You've come a long way, baby." I walked into the drugstore and nervously plunked two dollars on the counter, hoping it was enough; the clerk wordlessly pushed back one of the bills, then handed me two quarters, a nickel, and the pale yellow packet. Back in the car, I unpeeled the cellophane, yanked out the foil insert, and struggled to release the first cigarette. The pack then made the rounds to the three other girls in the car. Pulling the lighter out of the dashboard, I pressed the cigarette tip into the red-hot circle, inhaled, and started coughing. Soon all four of us were hacking.

"This is disgusting!" one of the girls shrieked. She opened the car door and stubbed the cigarette out on the pavement. The other two soon followed.

I tried to persevere, fighting the nausea rising in my throat. I had learned to like coffee and was determined to add this to my skills. How else would I be able to blow smoke rings? I got about halfway through the cigarette and gave up. Before we headed back, I tossed the rest of the pack into a trash can and checked the car for evidence, inspecting the floor mats and ashtray for telltale wrappers and butts. But the smell of cigarette smoke clung to the velour seats, so when I got home, I ran inside for some Lysol. After spraying the interior with a healthy dose, I showered and went to bed.

The next morning at breakfast, I warily watched my father walk out the front door, only to storm back in two minutes later.

"My car stinks," he barked. "Were you smoking?"

I couldn't lie my way out of this one. My face reddened.

"A little."

He shot me a significant look. "You better not do it again." At last, something we agreed on. I nodded sheepishly, realizing that my new pastime would have to be indulged al fresco.

My parents were more sanguine about drinking, as long as I did it where they could see. Lubavitcher men made the consumption of hard liquor at Shabbos and holiday meals as much a part of their religious practice as putting on tefillin every morning but, as with smoking, women were not expected to join in; we were limited to decorous sips of kiddush wine or toasts of Sabra liqueur at weddings. An occasional cocktail was also considered acceptable for the ladies. My mother liked to start a meal at Moshe Peking with a Tom Collins or a whiskey sour, and sometimes she would hand one of us the orange slice or the maraschino cherry. So when I took out the blender one night and whipped up a batch of piña coladas from the kosher frozen mix I'd discovered at the Stop & Shop, they were unconcerned, and even had a taste, out of curiosity. Of the kiddush wine pilfered from a school cabinet with a flimsy lock and the White Russians my friends and I consumed at Fitzwilly's downtown, they knew nothing.

Somewhere between the driving, smoking, and drinking, I studied. Dottie had embarked on a campaign to get us ready for college-level work. She got our English class advance-placement-accredited, put us on a strict diet of literary classics, and had us writing constantly, teaching us the difference among expository, creative, and critical composition. Eventually, I could do a reasonable job of teasing a theme out of a poem or novel, writing a strong opening paragraph, and structuring an analytical essay. I still labored over each piece—the crying jags were now embedded into my writing process—but sometimes a paragraph or phrase would sing so elegantly, I would sit back and wonder where it had come from. Dottie's comments grew more encouraging. "Like the best of Art Buchwald!" she gushed over a pert fable on turtle racing, and my heart swelled. I did well in my other classes, but for her I wanted to *shine*.

I finally broached the subject of college with my parents, and with surprisingly little argument they agreed to let me apply to Stern College. The school was all female, acceptably Modern Orthodox, and the joke was that most of the students were there to pursue their "MRS" degrees. My parents appreciated that I needed to do something to keep my brain functioning, and attending Stern, in and of itself, would probably not compromise my marriage prospects. It went without saying that I was not cut out to be the wife of a Torah scholar, and as long as I kept my reputation lily-white, I could still find a nice Lubavitcher boy who was "in business," like my father. My mother and I took the train into Manhattan one afternoon to visit the school. We met with the dean of admissions for a brief interview and then went to inspect the dorm a few blocks away. Chattering girls streamed in and out of the lobby, books clasped to their chests. Most wore skirts, but I also saw a few in jeans. To our right was a lounge, where a handful of Modern Orthodox boys in crocheted yarmulkes had settled into puffy couches, waiting for girls to come down from their dorm rooms. No males were allowed upstairs, the security guard assured us. My mother found this very encouraging. I was somewhat less enthusiastic. Not counting the boys in the lounge, the scene reminded me of the Lubavitcher camp in California. The campus of my dreams this was not.

I knew that a coed university was off the table, as was any college not in New York or somewhere close to New Haven. Nonetheless, I spent an afternoon in the library researching women's colleges in Massachusetts and wrote away for information on Mount Holyoke, Smith, and Simmons. At the same time, catalogs arrived in the mail almost daily from schools I had never heard of—Rensselaer Polytechnic Institute, College of the Holy Cross, Case Western Reserve, and Miami University, inexplicably transplanted to Ohio. Glossy photographs showcased wholesome students relaxing cross-legged on lush lawns, poring over volumes in low-lit libraries, or peering at test tubes through safety goggles. The professors always looked thoughtful and buttoned up, save one scruffy male waving his arms in front of a chalkboard filigreed with mathematical formulas. At Sweet Briar College, hale young women apparently spent their days astride majestic horses, pensively surveying the Virginia landscape. What would they make, I wondered, of a wavy-haired Hasidic feminist whose preferred form of contact with animals was on a dinner plate?

Even more extraordinary were the course lists: Origins of Human Society, Introduction to Astrophysics, The Novel and Psychoanalysis, Political Philosophy, Francophone Cinema. I hungered for all of them. I could see my father shaking his head over the uselessness of studying Victorian poetry—*why can't you read it on your own?*—but to me these classes were portals to an intellectual heaven. I obsessively thumbed through the growing stack in my bedroom, and the more I studied them, the more real college began to seem to me.

"You'll go to Barnard, of course," Dottie said. We were in her office, discussing applications and personal essays. She'd smirked when I mentioned my visit to Stern. Barnard was Dottie's alma mater. I had gone through their catalog, but it seemed too far out of reach.

"I don't think I'd get in," I protested. "It's part of Columbia. And no one there has even heard of our school."

"Don't be ridiculous. You'll do fine."

"But what'll I write about?" I felt myself tearing up with fear and frustration. As far as wearing down my parents, Barnard was in the outer realm of the possible; it was all women and in New York. But it was too much to hope that I might actually be admitted.

In the end, I applied to Barnard and Stern. For my parents' educational backgrounds, I made my father's time spent learning in *kollel* and his rabbinic ordination sound as much as possible like graduate school. Dottie and two other teachers wrote glowing letters of recommendation. Pondering my personal essay, I tried to excavate something interesting about myself from the past seventeen years. I was reluctant to reveal my Hasidic background, certain that it would conjure an image of a mousy, thick-stockinged, long-skirted, benighted, and insulated teenager, which, although closer to the truth than not, was not how I wished to present myself. In the end, I spun a classic immigrant's tale: refugee parents seeking a better life for their family and imparting solid American values to their children, their joy at my being the first to go to college, and so on. That my grandparents had more in common with sectarian Puritans seeking religious freedom than with immigrants who flocked to Ellis Island for America's gold-paved streets went unmentioned, as did the fact that my parents had grave concerns about releasing their restless, impressionable offspring into what they considered the maw of corruption. I had not even told them I was applying to Barnard. In the end, the essay read like inspirational fiction, finely crafted paragraphs that bore no resemblance to the truth. I was too embarrassed by it to show it to anyone, including Dottie. Instead, in early January I slipped the essay into an envelope along with the application forms and quietly sent it off.

Then I began to look for a propitious time to soften the ground with my parents. One night, when they were in the family room watching television in their matching Naugahyde armchairs (another perk from the Deitsch plastics factory), I settled myself on the carpet and leaned against my mother's ottoman.

When the commercials came on, I turned to face them. "So, I was thinking it would be great to go to Barnard, if I got in," I said. "I applied."

"I know," my mother said. "I saw it in my checkbook." I often signed my mother's name to her checks, with her approval, to pay my piano teacher or the dry cleaner. Out of habit, I'd written a check for the thirty-five-dollar application fee and entered it into her register without thinking that she would see it before I was ready to go public.

"So, what do you think?" I held my breath.

She raised her eyebrows a bit. "I'm worried that you won't stay *frum*. I think you're looking for a way out of being religious."

Well, they certainly nailed that one. I immediately went on the defensive.

"No, I'm not!" I protested. "It's a good school. And Dottie thinks I'll have no problem getting in."

It was the wrong thing to say.

"I don't give a damn *what* she thinks," my mother said, her voice rising. "She's trying to influence you girls to become *apikorsim*, plain and simple." She paused. "You know she's a terrible person."

My parents were not the only ones who mistrusted Dottie. She came off as arrogant and patronizing in parent-teacher meetings, and her antireligious, "opiate of the masses" views, while never articulated in front of the parents, were reported back to them by some of the kids. Many of the Orthodox parents had complained about her to Rabbi Hirschman, who counseled patience. It's not easy to find teachers willing to work for what we can afford to pay, he would say. No one could argue with that.

I guiltily leapt to Dottie's defense and tried to bring the conversation back to the subject at hand.

"Why do you blame everything on her?" I shouted. "Maybe I *want* to go, maybe it was *my* idea! What's wrong with getting a good education for once?"

"There's nothing wrong with it," my mother said, "but you're a Lubavitcher girl and college can be very tempting. You also have a reputation to consider."

"Barnard has lots of *frum* students," I argued. "And they have a kosher kitchen. Ariella's sister went there." Ariella's older sister had, indeed, attended Barnard and emerged not only unscathed but engaged to a dentist. I was crying now, pleading but still furious.

My mother was silent, then turned to my father.

"Say something, please."

"What's wrong with Stern?" he asked.

"It's not as good a school as Barnard. Everybody knows that. Besides, all you care about is what other people think! What about your children? Aren't we important?"

That hit a nerve with my father, as I'd hoped it would. "What are you talking about? Of course we care."

"You have to remember that you're not alone in this world," my mother insisted. "We're part of a community, with standards. And fair or not, people are going to judge you by what you do." She looked as though she was about to cry, too.

She was making reasonable arguments, of course. They just no longer applied to me. And I couldn't simply come out and say it. This was clearly going nowhere.

"That's a bunch of crap!" I shouted. I stomped out and ran

upstairs to my room, slamming the door behind me. Directly below, I heard the urgent murmur of their conversation. Pressing my ear to the floor, I tried to listen but couldn't make out the words. I sat up and noticed a toy my sister Suri had left behind. It was a Fisher-Price See 'n Say, ringed with pictures of farm animals. It was hefty, and a little smaller than the steering wheel of a car. I raised it over my head and smashed it to the floor.

"Hey!" my father yelled. That came through loud and clear.

A few minutes later, there was a soft knock at the door. It was Ricki.

"Are you okay?" she asked.

"Mom and Dad are so horrible."

She nodded. "I know. They just don't get it."

I was grateful for her sympathy. Ricki and I had spent most of our childhood bickering. Less than two years apart, we each attempted to stake out our own identities. I was the academic who loved playing the piano and had an endless appetite for shopping; Ricki, the artist who took ballet classes and was always involved in an ambitious crafts project. In reality, we had always been more in sync than we cared to admit and, putting aside the petty arguments, we were tightly bound together. As Lubavitcher teenagers living in the Connecticut outback, we often felt as though we belonged nowhere, and our shared desire to escape the confines of Hasidic life had brought us closer. Just shy of sixteen, Ricki hoped to go to art school when she graduated, which was going to be an even tougher sell to my parents than Barnard. Soon, she would be in my shoes—broken in by me, of course. If my parents had meant for me to set an example for my younger sisters, I was doing so in ways that they had never anticipated. Fortunately, any further conversations about Barnard could be put off until the end of March, when I would find out whether or not I had been accepted.

Trying to fill the time until the notifications arrived in the mail, I hit pay dirt when Bubby Deitsch lent me her little blue Saab while she and my grandfather went to Florida for the winter. Although that meant assuming morning carpool duty for my sisters, I could also skip out of school during lunch if for nothing other than a candy run to the nearby Wawa market. Maintaining a car—getting it washed, gassing it up—made me feel grown-up and independent. In the evenings, after dropping off my friends, I would drive around alone for a while longer—through snowy back roads, near the deserted shore of the Long Island Sound, anywhere quiet enough to let my mind drift. I tried to imagine what life at Barnard would be like, transposing Yale's ivy-covered buildings onto the unknown precincts of upper Manhattan. I was always gabbing in these scenes, the words indistinct but clearly brilliant and witty: sitting on a bench on the quad as I argued with friends about the finer points of Greek philosophy, gesturing to emphasize a point in class as I impressed the professor with my interpretation of the text in question, parsing the meaning of the foreign film I'd just seen with my boyfriend who, with his mop of dark hair, Jewish nose, and round glasses, bore a slightly handsomer resemblance to George S. Kaufman.

Only occasionally would I let come to the surface the fear that had burrowed deep inside me. In actuality, I was painfully self-conscious around strangers and had never really had to make new friends. What if I was the dumbest one there? Would any guy even look at me, or would they all be repelled by an invisible electrified Hasid fence, an aura of weirdness that I would never be able to shed? During these more somber reality checks, when I pictured myself in the dining hall, on the quad, or in class, I sat tongue-tied, an interloper trying to sneak past the velvet rope. When I tried to repress these images, my insomnia, which had gone into brief remission, returned with a vengeance. I was subsisting on three hours of sleep a night and heavy infusions of caffeine.

A bright spot on the horizon was our upcoming family trip to Israel—my first—which had been planned for March. Zaydie Deitsch had always dreamed of opening a branch of the family business there, and a few years earlier my aunt and uncle had pulled up stakes in Crown Heights, moved to Israel, and gotten things started. The new factory was now up and running, and we planned to both visit our relatives and tour the country. I was particularly excited about a promised excursion to Masada. The story of the small band of Jewish rebels who committed mass suicide there in 73 CE rather than surrender to the Roman army was utterly devastating. Having read Yigal Yadin's account of the excavation he led in the mid-1960s, I wanted to see for myself the artifacts pictured in the book, the pots and leather sandals that made the lives of these martyrs real and immediate. I readied the list of souvenirs I'd bring back from the trip: a silver ring with my name engraved on it in Hebrew letters, my own leather sandals, an embroidered Shabbos caftan from the Arab souk in Jerusalem, and Hebrew Coca-Cola T-shirts for my friends. And I couldn't wait to encounter all those handsome Israeli soldiers I'd seen on the news.

Then one evening about two weeks before the trip, my father found me in the living room and sat down next to me.

"I have some bad news, *maicheleh.*" This was an endearment he'd stopped using since I'd become a raving teenage lunatic. I sat up and looked at him warily.

"What happened?"

"Israel is off."

I couldn't believe it.

"But *what happened*?" I repeated, my heart pounding.

"We got an answer back from the Rebbe."

I had a feeling I knew where this was headed.

"We sent him a letter, just asking for a *brachah*. It's a long trip, so we thought it couldn't hurt."

"*And?*"

"And the way he answered, we think it's better not to go."

I still couldn't absorb what he was telling me. The Rebbe had said no, like some stony-faced customs official, and now we weren't going? It seemed crazy. Why had they even written to him in the first place? Shock was slowly being replaced by fury.

"So if he didn't specifically say 'no,' what the hell did he say?"

My father let the curse word ride. I could see he felt terrible.

"It was something to do with the cost of the trip. It might not look right, he said, it could send the wrong message. I'm sorry, *maicheleh.* We're all disappointed."

I was more than disappointed. I felt as though I'd been slapped hard, not just by the loss of the trip, but also by the stark realization of my larger, more existential predicament. No matter how many subversive novels and record albums I consumed, no matter how many jangly earrings I poked into my earlobes, through my veins would always course Hasidic blood, and there was no transfusion that would ever rid me of it. I belonged to a tribe of parents, grandparents, aunts, uncles, and cousins, all of whom accepted without question the word of the Rebbe, or at least accepted enough of what he said to stick to the boundaries he set for them. What would happen if they decided to ask the Rebbe for a blessing for Barnard?

"It's not fair, Dad! Why can't we go anyhow?" A dumb question, which he didn't bother answering.

I tried to salvage the last crumbs of my belief in the Rebbe's supernatural prescience. The day after we were meant to leave for Tel Aviv, I searched for news of an El Al plane crash. There wasn't even a hijacking. Perhaps over the next two weeks the Palestine Liberation Organization would attack a group of tourists, or the Jerusalem Plaza would go up in flames. All was calm, according to the papers. Although I knew I was being ridiculous, part of me hoped for a sign of our own personal miracle—that the Rebbe had foreseen danger in our path and shoved us off it just in the nick of time. When what was to have been our return flight landed safely at JFK, I shut the door on him for good.

The packet from Barnard was waiting on my bed one afternoon when I came home from school. A packet meant I'd been admitted! I ripped it open. "We are delighted to inform you—" the letter began, and I pressed it close to my chest. I couldn't stop smiling. I riffled through the forms and brochures, trying to make sense of all the information about deadlines, dorms, meal plans, course requirements, advisers, libraries, and getting around safely in New York City. My eyes widened when I got to the part that spelled out how much everything was going to cost. I needed to respond by mid-April. I flew downstairs to the kitchen.

"Hey, I got in, Mommy!" I waved the letter.

"I figured." She was smiling, too. "But I need to talk to Dad about it."

When my father came home, I shared the news with him excitedly, pretending that I didn't know my mother had called him as soon as the mail had come. He couldn't even fake enthusiasm.

"We'll talk about it," he said, grimly.

The next morning, I found Dottie in her office.

"Barnard said yes!" I shouted. "I did it!"

Dottie came from behind her desk to give me a hug. She was beaming, too.

"Of course you did."

"I still can't believe it! Thank you so much, Dottie."

We talked a bit about what classes I would take and about college life in New York. Dottie, who had gone to Barnard in the late fifties and early sixties, described the thrill of all-night sessions at Beat coffeehouses and jazz clubs. She did not mention my parents or ask how they'd taken the news, and I volunteered nothing. I felt bad enough about colluding with the person my parents regarded as the enemy. There was no need for me to give her an opportunity to skewer them or to simply dismiss them and their concerns.

That night, my parents laid out the terms and conditions. I could go to Barnard but I had to promise to join Hillel, a national organization of Jewish college students. I would come home every Shabbos. And I would need to defer for a year and go to seminary. Unspoken, nonnegotiable, and understood was that I was to stay *frum,* no matter what.

"We're trusting you to do the right thing," my mother said. I swore I would and hugged them both, choosing not to see the worry in their eyes. I wanted to stay happy.

"Oh, thank you, thank you! Are you going to tell Bubby and Zaydie?" I was eager to share the good news.

"Of course," my father said wryly. "How can we not?" He knew better than to expect congratulatory backslaps.

The seminary requirement was a reasonable one. Many Orthodox girls continued their Jewish studies for a year or two after high school graduation. Most of the seminary programs gave girls the option to acquire a license for teaching Jewish subjects in yeshivas, but they went for a variety of reasons. Some were looking for something to keep them occupied while they waited to get married, some had a genuine intellectual or religious interest in higher education, and still others just thought it would make them look good to the matchmakers. Each institution tended to have its own character, and of course the Lubavitchers had their own network of seminaries. The Bais Rivkah Seminary in Crown Heights, for example, attracted girls who had office jobs in the city or who were about to get engaged and needed to be near home. The other large Lubavitcher seminary, in Israel, had a stricter code of personal conduct and a more rigorous curriculum. Because Orthodox American teenagers were considered, for the most part, to be "wild," few American girls were accepted to the Israel program. This was fine with me, and the idea of living in Crown Heights and attending seminary there was too painful to contemplate. I got no pushback from my parents on that score. They wanted my seminary experience to be a positive one—perhaps so positive that I would abandon the idea of Barnard. Or, even better, I

might get engaged during my seminary year and, with my reputation intact, I could then attend college without their having to
suffer the Lubavitcher community's slings and arrows. I considered non-Lubavitcher Orthodox seminaries in Jerusalem. Some
catered to a more modern crowd, which I knew would make my
parents unhappy. Others attracted slightly older students or those
of a more scholarly bent, while still others were meant for *ba'alei
teshuvah* looking for a crash course in the basics of Torah and
Jewish law.

Then I heard about the seminary in Gateshead, England, from
Tzip, who was planning to go there. Tucked away in the very
north of the country, it was known to be extremely *frum,* she said,
but she was fine with that, and her cousin, an old camp friend of
mine, was thinking of going, too. The idea of having friends at
seminary squelched my concern about too many rules. I was also
intrigued by the idea of living in England, conjuring Shakespeare,
Thomas Hardy, Agatha Christie, Catherine awaiting Heathcliff
on the moors, not to mention my beloved Mick Jagger. When I
mentioned Gateshead to my mother, her eyes lit up.

"Oh, that's supposed to be an excellent program," she said
enthusiastically. "It's been around since I was young." She paused.
"I hear it's hard to get into." I couldn't tell whether she was refer-
ring to their high educational or religious standards. She called the
school's New York office for an application and several weeks later,
we once again took the train into Manhattan for an interview. I
made sure to go for the "full *tznius,*" leaving off the bright lipstick
and replacing my denim skirt with a long, somber dark gabar-
dine, which I paired with a high-necked, long-sleeved blouse, non-
descript hose, and low pumps. My free-flowing hair was pulled

back into a tight French braid. We were greeted in the hallway by a well-dressed, obviously *frum* woman who smiled warmly, shook our hands, and led us into a small office. I noticed my application on her desk; notes had been scribbled in the margins.

"Well, Chaya, your teachers all speak very highly of you," she said, as my mother beamed and nodded. "So tell me why you'd like to come to Gateshead." I spoke glowingly of the school's storied reputation for rigorous learning and how important that was to me. Now it was her turn to nod. As an alumna of the seminary, she could not agree more: the camaraderie of the girls, the brilliance of the rabbis, the intensity with which Jewish philosophy was taught and experienced—all of it, she said, combined to make Gateshead the legendary place that it was.

"I came away with such a deep appreciation of *yiddishkeit,* it's still with me," she said. "I can honestly say those were some of the happiest years of my life."

I asked about the other students. Where were they from? Most of the girls were English, she said, but there were some French and Israeli girls, too. There were not too many Americans, she said primly; the school was careful about who they accepted. It was technically a three-year program, but most girls stayed for two years, dropping out when they got engaged. How long did I plan to stay? she asked. Oh, at least two years, I reassured her. I knew what I had to say.

The acceptance letter arrived a week later. Classes were to begin in mid-August. I would have to send them a record of my vaccinations and a chest X-ray before I arrived. The school would take care of obtaining my student visa when I got there. Also included with the letter was an extensive list of books I had to bring with me, which included Bibles with commentary, compilations of Jewish law, a book of Psalms, and a Hebrew-English dictionary. My father wrote away to a bookseller in Crown Heights for them. I was relieved when he teased me about writing to the Rebbe for a double blessing. Between the non-Lubavitcher seminary and the even more verboten college, we both knew where that would get us.

II

A Girl in Sem

My mother and I spent the summer amassing a wardrobe of "good" clothing to replace my denim skirts, peasant blouses, and over-sized vests. Gateshead had a conservative reputation, not just in religious matters but also in what it considered proper dress, manners, and behavior—what my mother approvingly called "European." Repeat trips to Loehmann's and Macy's yielded woolen A-line skirts that extended unflatteringly down to the middle of my calves; merino cardigans with pearlescent buttons; lace-bibbed flannel nightgowns; a duster that zipped all the way up to my neck to relax in; and a dozen packs of plain nylons and tights. For Shabbos wear I selected a dressy suit with a modest but perky peplum jacket. Not knowing what was available in England, we also loaded up on twelve months' worth of my favorite brands of shampoo, soap, toothpaste, tampons, and razors. When my parents and sisters saw me off at JFK, I was surrounded by five brand-new yellow Samsonite suitcases that had been stuffed with my mother's vision of the perfect Gateshead wardrobe: sedate, ladylike outfits that would not have been out of place at tea with the queen. I left my mother sobbing at the gate and joined the other Americans on their way to the seminary—Tzip, her cousin, and a girl who had just flown in from Detroit. I was nervous but excited.

In my imagination, the word "Gateshead" suggested a large Gothic stone building, dignified yet welcoming, surrounded by a playing field and formal English gardens, with a pond and benches for reading Penguin Classics. But when our taxi deposited us at the door of the seminary (to my humiliation, we needed a second car just for my luggage), I beheld no estate upon the shires, but, instead, something closer to Lowood Institution from *Jane Eyre*. Standing on the pavement, I took in with some dismay the gray row houses that would serve as my bedroom, classroom, and dining room for the next year. An old church glowered at us from across the street.

Entering the main door at 50 Bewick Road, we were met by a middle-aged woman with a stiff *sheitel* and no-nonsense attitude who checked us off a list and directed us to different rooms. I passed through dingy, wallpapered corridors and finally reached a room containing eight narrow beds separated by small wooden nightstands. It looked like an army barracks. A few girls who'd arrived earlier were chattering away in clipped British accents. They stopped talking to silently watch as I claimed a bed under a window with a view of the church, and then resumed their conversation. Still punchy from the flight (we'd landed at six that morning), I barely registered the snub and set about unpacking. I looked for the closets, but all I could find was a single built-in wardrobe that extended along the far wall, with a curtain instead of a door. It was obviously meant for all eight of us, but my clothing alone would probably take up about half of it. My roommates were all wearing some variation of what appeared to be the unofficial Gateshead uniform: pastel button-down cotton shirt, dark skirt, and sensible shoes. No one wore makeup that I could tell. I picked through my suitcases for the plainest clothes I could find, relegating the rest to the attic for storage.

Our freshman class—referred to as "T3," the first year in the countdown to the end of the three-year program—numbered about 120. The weekly schedule at "Sem," as the seminary was called by everyone, had been codified when the school was established, in the early 1950s, by Emmanuel Kohn, a German Jew who had fled the Nazis and who still held the reins as headmaster. Each day, morning prayers were followed by a serve-yourself breakfast of toast and cereal in the dining room. (The milk was not homogenized; if you were the first to unseal a bottle, you could spoon off the cream that had risen to the top into your coffee.) We then filed into a classroom, took our assigned seats, and at 9:00 a.m. sharp the door would open, we'd rise, and the first in a succession of rabbis would enter, motion for us to sit, and proceed to deliver a rote lecture on the Bible, the prophets, Jewish law and history, or education. Although the lectern came equipped with a seating chart, few of our teachers bothered to learn our names. At noon, we trooped back to the dining room for a hot lunch that was as predictable as our classes. Sunday: vegetable soup, cold cuts, string beans, mashed potatoes, and apples. Monday: split-pea soup, goulash, carrots and peas, mashed potatoes, and apples. And so on. Then back into the classroom for one or two similarly uninspiring afternoon classes, homework with an assigned study partner, and the school day came to an end. A cold supper was served at six and lights-out was at eleven. We had Wednesdays and Sunday afternoons off. On Friday afternoons, girls could volunteer to help one of the local housewives prepare for Shabbos. The rest of us were on our own.

I spent my free time in those early weeks writing letters to everyone I knew. Aunts, grandparents, friends, cousins, forgotten bunkmates from camp, even my old piano teacher. All received amusing, lighthearted letters that I hoped would make them write back. I never wrote to Dottie. By encouraging me to apply to Barnard, she had thrown me a lifeline and I'd gratefully grabbed at it, but at the same time I felt sick at how upset this had made my family. So I tried to vaporize her from my consciousness, which of course made me feel guilty and ungrateful. I owed Dottie so much, but I felt that maintaining contact with her would be an additional betrayal of my parents.

I also explored the town of Gateshead, often with the other American girls in my class. It seemed to specialize in bad weather and ugly architecture, although we eventually discovered the English park of my imaginings, complete with walking paths and a rose garden. Invariably, we ended up on Coatsworth Road, the main Jewish drag, which was lined with grocery stores, bakeries, butcher shops, drugstores, hardware stores, and boutiques that sold appropriately modest clothing for the *frum* community. We learned a lesson in manners one day when, snacking on cookies we'd just bought, we were approached by an older man who gave us a disgusted look and a lecture on the vulgarity of eating on the street.

We were warned to give wide berth to the gentile population, whom the Jews referred to simply as the "English." It was 1981, two years after Margaret Thatcher took office and broke the backs of the labor unions. Recession had hit the northeast particularly hard, putting thousands out of work and making the cloistered, self-sufficient Jewish community a particular target of hatred. Bands of teenagers would drive past us in the street, shouting, "Dirty Jews!" Many of the local men spent their days at the pub next to the church. Weaving home in the early evening, they serenaded us as they passed, belting out songs that in their knotty Geordie accents sounded like sinister gibberish. All they needed were torches and belted tunics, and their resemblance to the Russian peasants who had terrorized my great-grandparents would be complete.

I tried to submit to the rigidity of school, or at least find some humor in it, but it wasn't easy. I felt trapped and alone, and most of the handful of American girls in my class seemed equally shell-shocked. The English girls were younger than we were—most had left high school at sixteen, after O levels—and thoroughly unaware of the outside world. When I attempted to explain the meaning of the phrase "spaced out" to my first study partner, Estie, a pasty redhead from London, she looked at me blankly, and no amount of context could enlighten her. The French and Israeli students seemed somewhat more worldly, but they tended to keep to themselves. They generally spoke little English, making me wonder what they could possibly have gotten out of our classes. Most impressive were the Swiss girls, who spoke four or five languages fluently, but whose formal manners made them hard nuts to crack socially.

The school year began in the Hebrew month of Elul, a period of prayer and atonement that leads up to Rosh Hashanah. The

Gateshead crowd took it particularly seriously. Most of the community identified with the *Musar* movement, an educational and ethical approach to religious observance that had been founded in nineteenth-century Lithuania. Unlike Hasidism, with its joyful and mystical approach to religious observance, the *Musar* approach demanded discipline and self-reflection. During morning prayers, I noticed the girls around me mouthing each word deliberately and slowly as they concentrated on the meaning and purpose of every sentence in the prayer book. Used to racing through *davening*, I tried to slow myself down, but it was like trying to savor overcooked broccoli; inevitably I would rush to the finish and be forced to wait while everyone else caught up. Thoughtful prayer was just one of the *midos,* or good character traits, that my classmates actively worked on. When I wisecracked to a roommate about someone's unattractive sweater, her eyes widened in horror.

"That's *loshen hora!*" she gasped and turned away. Yes, it was idle gossip, or, literally, evil speech, something that, back home, we were generally instructed to avoid, but no one had ever made that big a deal about it. This was my first encounter with hellfire-and-brimstone Judaism. It felt like a different religion. Every evening that month, we gathered for post-supper sermons on sin, repentance, and the mortification of our baser natures. The lectures, thunderously delivered by our rabbis, hooked us with a story, more often than not a parable about a king of an unnamed country. Sometimes he is punished for his arrogance or evil designs; other times the king is God, and the moral is that we, His subjects, must serve and submit. Passages from the scripture would be pulled in like threads and woven into blistering reprimands about our own wickedness and insufficient fear of heaven. The period from Rosh

Hashanah to Yom Kippur, known as the Ten Days of Repentance, was even more intense; there were often two lectures each night, filled with rhetoric even fiercer and more ominous. It was assumed that by the time Yom Kippur finally arrived, in early October, we would be properly abject and primed for atonement. And, if our prayers were sufficiently sincere, we would be forgiven for the sins of the previous year and inscribed in the Book of Life for the coming year. Given the seriousness of the day, on Yom Kippur we didn't pray at school but with the larger Jewish community at one of the three shuls in Gateshead. Services began at seven a.m. and went straight through until sundown, when the fast ended. The two-hour afternoon break, a staple of pretty much every shul I was familiar with, was nowhere in evidence here. I didn't know how I would make it through the day. At some point in the afternoon I looked over at my American friend standing next to me, who in turn pointed to one of our classmates. She was swaying from side to side, her eyes closed, siddur clasped to her chest, and she was weeping, as were a number of other girls around us.

"Why is it that the best girls always feel the worst?" I whispered.

"I don't know, but I'm starving," she said, before we were shushed by one of the local ladies in our row.

Our fall break started the next day. I was headed to Israel at last, to visit relatives as well as my friend Jordana, who was now a freshman at Hebrew University. My aunt met me at the airport, and as we drove through Tel Aviv, with its vibrant street life, I felt as though a mist had lifted. The six weeks I had spent in gray and gloomy England seemed like a memory of someone else's life.

My aunt and her family lived in a small city south of Tel Aviv, in a neighborhood populated largely by Russian immigrants and Lubavitchers. My immersion in Sem's Lithuanian rigidity made the Hasidim around me seem blessedly tolerant and joyously materialistic. On furlough for the next three weeks, I was determined to make the most of my freedom—to travel where I pleased, eat what I liked, go about stocking-free, and flirt with handsome soldiers. I'd been warned that Israeli men assumed all American girls were easy, and my Hebrew was just good enough to get me into trouble. At a bus stop near my aunt's house, a young man in fatigues sidled up to me. Olive-skinned and with a trim build, close-cropped black hair, and an Uzi slung across his chest, he was the Israeli soldier of my dreams.

"Shalom," he said, smiling at me.

"Shalom," I replied, smiling back.

He said something incomprehensible. I shrugged my shoulders. *"Lo miveenah,"* I said. *I don't understand.* He asked if I knew French, and I nodded enthusiastically. This was fun. But he wasn't able to make any headway there, either—*"Je ne comprend pas"* was all I could manage to mumble—and so he switched back to Hebrew, looking more and more frustrated. Finally, I latched on to a familiar word and realized he was politely asking whether he could feel me up. I blushed and just as politely sent him on his way.

I left my aunt to spend a few days with Jordana in Jerusalem, camping out in her dorm room. She'd enrolled in a special program for Americans, which seemed to entail little more than a few classes each week and some light reading. She spent the bulk of her time going out with friends—mostly young Americans and

Europeans—drinking coffee at the sidewalk cafés on Ben Yehuda Street and watching foreign films at the art house cinema. Tagging along, I envied the ease of it all—the banter, the political debates, the accepted flirtations between the men and women. They were mostly Modern Orthodox and wore their religious observance lightly. If they ever wondered where on the religious continuum they belonged, they could just look to their parents or to their high school classmates back home. Their lives seemed so much more straightforward than mine. They weren't constantly struggling to fit in somewhere, as I was.

Why had I ever thought Gateshead would be fun?

The three weeks flew by too quickly. I left Israel in a miserable state. Landing at Gatwick late on a Sunday night, I caught the last train back to Newcastle, a run-down milk train that would double the usual four-hour ride. The conductor dimmed the lights so the passengers could sleep and I cried most of the way—grieving for the poor choice I'd made and furious at my fate.

My mother wrote at least once a week, filling thin airmail pages with family news and details of her days. Occasionally, she included small scraps of paper filled with crayoned lines of color—contributions from my four-year-old sister, Suri—that landed on the table like snowflakes when I shook them out of the envelope. I imagined my other sisters and her sitting down to supper after school, complaining about teachers and fighting over the last drumstick. I wondered who was bullying them into doing their chores and whether they were glad I was gone. I missed watching my favorite TV shows and, perhaps more painfully, listening to my beloved record collection. I'd made tapes of the essentials—the Rolling Stones, James Taylor, Heart, Billy Joel—and hid them in a shoe box under my bed. After lights-out, I'd burrow beneath my blanket, slip on the headphones of my Walkman, and, keeping the volume as low as possible, gently press the Play button so that it didn't click.

Eventually, I began to get used to life at Sem. A new underground began running that winter, linking Gateshead to Newcastle, just across the Tyne River. Now, on Wednesday afternoons, a few of us would head to the main shopping district in Newcastle, where we poked through Boots and WHSmith looking for British odds and ends—Denman brushes, A4 notebooks, and fountain pens. I also discovered the local public library and, under the alias Yvonne Hauptman (appropriated from a glamorous girl back in high school), applied for a card and borrowed *The Brothers Karamazov* and *A Portrait of the Artist as a Young Man,* which went under the bedcovers, too.

I also made my first good friend at school. Monica had grown up in the San Fernando Valley and, in the reverse of my own situation, had disappointed her secular, comfortably situated parents by becoming ultra-Orthodox on a youth-group trip to Israel. As a rule, Gateshead was reluctant to accept newly observant girls—that was left for the Lubavitchers—but Monica's rabbi in Jerusalem was highly respected and a close friend of Mr. Kohn, and he had put in a good word for her. In fact, she had proven to be a pretty quick study of *frum* ways, with few indicators that she was actually a *ba'alas teshuvah.* She spoke and read flawless Hebrew and in only a few years had managed to absorb enough knowledge of scripture, Jewish law, and philosophy to sound as though she'd been yeshiva-trained since childhood. Her English had even taken on the slight Talmudic singsong associated with the most studious yeshiva boys. She'd arranged a dozen baseball-card-size photos of famous rabbis in the shape of a fan on the wall behind her bed, from which location they grimly surveyed a girlish tableau of nightgowns and flowered coverlets. If anything identified Monica's status as a latecomer to observance, it was her attire. Reared in jeans, she was under the impression that being *frum* relegated one to a wardrobe of long, unflattering pleated skirts, severe blouses, and expensively sturdy Etienne Aigner loafers that not even my grandmother, let alone my mother, would wear. But despite her sincere religiosity, Monica was as bored with Sem as I was. At night, we would sit on her bed eating chocolate-covered mints— unlike me, she never seemed to gain weight—and talk about our families; we often laughed so hard that I would feel sick afterward.

One thing that Monica had not been able to shake was a rebellious streak—an almost instinctive bucking against authority. But that was precisely why I loved her. Instead of opening an account at the local Lloyd's, where by unspoken rule Sem girls always banked, she went to Barclay's, which had been designated for the young men studying at the yeshiva on the other side of Coatsworth. During our twenty-minute class break she would sprint to Bloom's grocery, buy a fresh supply of sweets, and race back, slipping into her seat seconds before our teacher entered the room. I began joining her on these supply runs and we grew more and more daring, making the longer dash to Danskys and purchasing food that would be harder to hide. One day we bought ice cream cones, which we tried to eat as we ran back. We missed the bell, and as we skulked back to our seats we were greeted with murmurs of disapproval from the rest of the class.

Miraculously, Monica and I were assigned adjoining seats that second term. There being no exams at Gateshead, neither of us felt compelled to pay attention to the lectures. Instead, we spent class time playing Scrabble and Mastermind on mini board games hidden in our laps; sometimes Monica would embroider cloth napkins on a hoop hidden in her lap while I drew cartoons of our teachers for her amusement.

As close as I felt to Monica, I had to screw up my courage to tell her about Barnard. When I did, she was incredulous, and even angrier than I'd feared.

"How can you even *think* of going?" she said. "College is a place of *tuma.*" I cringed at the biblical word that meant "impure," "unclean."

"There are tons of Jews in college," I protested. "Religious Jews."

"You'll never stay *frum,*" she said, staring straight at me. "I know you. You're not strong enough to fight temptation."

"Of course I am." It sounded lame even as I said it. She certainly had me pegged—I didn't intend to fight temptation. Neither of us brought up the subject again, but it lingered, invisibly, like a bad odor.

Our second break came in early January, and I flew down to London to meet my parents, who would be visiting for a week. Watching them make their way through customs at Heathrow, my entire body relaxed; I felt as though I'd been holding my breath since August. I'd found a small kosher hotel in Golders Green, a Jewish neighborhood a short ride from the city center, where we would stay. My mother had filled one suitcase just with things for me: books and makeup I'd requested, a bag of my grandmother's chocolate chip cookies, cards from my sisters, and a small stack of mail, including a letter from Barnard requesting that I confirm by the end of the month my attendance the following fall.

Wanting to show my parents a good time, I'd planned a packed itinerary. We visited the usual tourist spots—Buckingham Palace, Big Ben, Hyde Park Corner, Harrods, and Madame Tussauds, where my father posed for a picture next to a wax figure of Lenin. At night, we saw *Amadeus* in the West End and had dinner at one of the kosher restaurants in Golders Green. My parents, not usually at ease in a new environment, seemed to be enjoying themselves, although they put their foot down at using the Tube. I'd made them take the train from the airport with their luggage, and they were still annoyed with me about it.

I'd been so excited about my parents' visit that I was unprepared for how angry and confused I would feel as the week went on. Strangely, the months I'd spent at Sem had only intensified how out of sync I felt with them, and it was doing odd things to me as well. In a city where religious Jews tended to stay in their own neighborhoods, I found myself embarrassed by the way they stuck out at all the tourist spots. But at the same time, their interests seemed so shallow compared to the religious hothouse that was Gateshead. I would snap at them and then feel ashamed of my meanness. I finally broke down on one of our last nights together, in a taxi on our way back to the hotel. My father was telling me about an old classmate who'd recently divorced his wife.

"Not that I'm surprised," he said, and then lowered his voice. "He was a bastard and she was a real . . . rhymes with 'witch.'"

"Dad, that's *rechilus,*" I said sternly. Slander was considered even worse than gossip. My father looked at my mother and the two of them burst out laughing. I was horrified.

"You're not allowed to!" I shrieked. "It's against the Torah—a real sin!"

I began to sob. They hustled me into their hotel room and tried to calm me down, but I couldn't stop. Panic and fury tumbled out of me, wailing accusations that carried through the corridor.

"Why do you do it?" I sobbed. "You know it's wrong!"

My mother sat me next to her on the bed and I leaned against her shoulder. My father stood there, looking helpless. He finally sat down, too.

"Not everything is black and white in this world," he said. "Everyone has their gray areas. Me, I would never rip open an envelope on Shabbos, but no one's perfect. Some things are easier to manage than other things. You just do the best you can. That's the way it is." It was the most open my father had ever been with me about religious observance—an invitation to share what I was feeling and, even more extraordinary, a promise that whatever I said would be okay. But I couldn't confide in him. I felt as though my tongue had been cut out. I simply nodded and went to my room, spent and remorseful. I wondered if I had gone crazy. The next morning, when my parents and I went down to breakfast, none of the other guests would meet our eyes. Our small hotel apparently had thin walls.

Back at Gateshead, I pulled out my Barnard confirmation form and carried it around with me for a week before filling it out: yes, I will attend. I took it to the post office to mail, praying that I wouldn't run into anyone from Sem and feeling like a spymaster forwarding instructions for a secret and perilous mission.

Meanwhile, engagement season for the British girls at Sem had officially begun. Almost daily, earsplitting shrieks of "Mazel tov!" and "Who is it?" rang through the halls on Bewick Road. On one day, five engagements were announced—a record for the year. They seemed to come out of nowhere. A girl would quietly slip away for a few days and return blushing and bearing new clothes and a gold watch that had been purchased by her future in-laws.

I was familiar with quick engagements—three-date courtships were not uncommon for Lubavitchers—but these existed in a totally different realm. Both sets of parents having previously met and approved of one another, the couple would then meet in the home of one of the two families for a few hours and decide, on the spot, whether to consent to the match or decline. Given the pressure to marry and the lack of knowledge about each other, most couples consented, trusting that their parents knew best. After a quick *l'chaim,* the boy and girl would not see each other again until their wedding, about three months later. The most religious girls, some as young as sixteen, would not even speak to their fiancés on the phone during this period. It was considered immodest.

Although dating wasn't allowed, marriage and children were a constant preoccupation among Sem students. Bridal catalogs were passed around and pored over, sparking animated discussions of fantasy weddings and dining room sets. One practical classmate, modeling a new coat, pulled at the extra fabric at the front. "See? Lots of room, so I won't have to buy another one when I get pregnant." Most of the girls were in fact shockingly ignorant regarding how these pregnancies would come about. One of the ladies in the Gateshead community gave the engaged Sem girls *kallah* classes, in which the laws of family purity and *mikvah* were taught, along with delicate allusions to what was in store for them in the bedroom. Rumor had it that some of the girls started crying or simply refused to believe what they were hearing. Late at night in our rooms, there were no gab sessions about boys or romance, let alone sex. Socializing of any sort between Sem girls and yeshiva boys simply didn't happen. The closest we came to a scandal that year was on Purim, a festive holiday during which it's actually a mitzvah for even normally abstemious men to get liquored up. With inebriated men stumbling in the streets, one of my classmates, a rabbi's daughter from Lichtenstein, daringly approached a young boy and asked him the time. Before she'd even returned to school, someone had reported the incident to Mr. Kohn, and by the next morning she was tearfully packing her bags, a cautionary tale for the rest of us.

We non-British Sem girls were mystified by this obsession with marriage. I imagined myself in some unfamiliar living room, trying to decide whether the nervous, wispy-bearded stranger seated next to me could be my lifelong bedmate, confidant, breadwinner, and children's father. What on earth would we talk about? While the thought was utterly depressing, if I was honest with myself, the idea of a defined, predictable role was oddly appealing; at least one knew what to do. Not to mention that I felt the pressure to yield to family expectations. My own romantic future I could envision only in cinematic flashes: sitting cross-legged on the lawn of a college quad, smoking and flirting; holding hands with a dazzlingly good-looking Jewish hunk; the two of us sitting with my parents, who in my fantasies are sometimes upset and sometimes give us their blessing. I had no alternative courtship models to look to; what I already knew, I didn't want. It was easier simply not to think about it for now. Otherwise, I might find myself shrieking, too, but for a different reason.

In the meantime, as the weeks went by and almost without

realizing it, I began falling under the Sem's spell. I still read my library books and kidded around with Monica. But I also grew more comfortable with the rules and routines. I auditioned for a part in the school's Tu B'Shevat holiday play and babysat for a local family, enjoying for the first time a sense of attachment to a large *frum* community. I started paying attention in class, absorbing Rabbi Fried's lessons on how properly to remove the pips from an orange on Shabbos (eat them with the fruit and spit them out, instead of picking them out first), and how many drops of milk would have to fall into a pot of chicken soup for the soup to become *trayf* (two parts milk into sixty parts chicken soup). I did my homework and discovered the intellectual satisfaction of deciphering the enigmatic medieval commentary surrounding the biblical texts. I even bought a dowdy gray flannel skirt and fussy ruffled white blouse at Marks & Spencer, and shocked my family by wearing them when I went home for Passover.

More unexpected was the urge to bolster my faith—to "work on myself," in Gateshead parlance—and thereby become a better Jew. I wanted Orthodox life to make sense to me. It would be so much easier that way. My family would be pleased, and I would find happiness both in believing as they believed and in receiving their approval. When I spoke to Monica about it, she got very excited and insisted I go talk to the rabbi who was our *musar* teacher.

"He's so smart," she said. "He really helped me when I had some problems." She didn't elaborate.

I was hesitant about taking her advice. This rabbi was the school's best teacher, a brilliant, charismatic speaker with a Scottish burr and sharp sense of humor. He seemed too intimidating to approach. I doubted he even knew who I was. But one day after class he asked if Chaya Deitsch could come up to the front. I made my way to him, my face reddening as all eyes followed me.

"I understand you'd like to come talk to me," he said.

I nodded. Monica's doing, obviously.

"Why don't you come to my house tomorrow afternoon, then—at two? The office has my address."

"Thank you."

I slept badly that night, trying to prepare for our conversation. I barely understood what I wanted myself, but maybe he could help me figure it out.

The rabbi's house was a ten-minute walk from school; it was a neat brick Tudor on a street I'd never seen. He answered the door, wearing a cardigan instead of the suit jacket he normally wore to class. He seemed surprised to see me.

"Hi, I'm Chaya. We had an appointment."

"Yes, I know. Come in," he said.

I followed him into his office, a small, dark room lined with books. He sat down at his desk and motioned to a chair opposite.

"So, what did you want to talk about?" he said softly. His expression was kindly, if a little detached.

"I'm . . . I'm having some . . . doubts," I said. "About believing."

"Believing what?"

I didn't know how to answer. The problem wasn't my shaky belief, it was that I didn't *want* to believe. That's what I needed to fix: I wanted to want to believe. I tried to say it without saying it. "Well, my heart's not in it. In doing mitzvahs and things."

"You believe in Hashem, don't you?" he asked.

"Oh, of course," I replied immediately.

"Then what you need is more *yiras shamayim*," he said. Fear of heaven. We were back to hellfire and brimstone. He looked at me, expectantly.

That was it? Do it or God will strike you down? I suddenly felt ridiculous. We were communicating across a chasm. The rabbi was on the side of faith and discipline, and I was on the side of— what? Self-indulgence and ingratitude. If I was able to follow his counsel, we wouldn't be having this conversation in the first place.

"Does that help?" he asked.

"I think so, yes," I lied.

My face betrayed my insincerity. "Are you sure?"

"Yes," I replied, a bit more decisively. I needed this conversation to end.

When I got back to Sem, Monica was waiting for me.

"So, isn't he great?" she said.

"Well, he gave me something to think about." I couldn't bear the idea of another tongue-lashing from her.

Not long after my meeting with the rabbi, Monica suddenly began to cool toward me. She spent more time with Tzip, who was fitting into Sem beautifully: studious, well liked, and taking to the grim austerity of the place as though she'd been born into it. Tzip and I kept up separately, because Monica was definitely not interested in a threesome. Although she and I still sat next to each other in class, we no longer played Scrabble or passed notes. When I came to see her in her room, she claimed to be tired. The rejection stung. I had no idea what I'd done wrong.

Late one afternoon I was alone in the classroom, finishing my homework. Glancing down, I noticed a letter sticking out of the cubby beneath Monica's desk. It was in her handwriting, on the graph paper she liked to use for correspondence. I was about to turn away when the word "friend" suddenly caught my eye. I pulled the sheet out. It was a letter to her rabbi in Israel asking for his help in resolving a Solomonic dilemma; she has two friends, she wrote, one whom she cares about deeply but who is a bad influence, and the other a girl of admirable moral character but with whom she is not as simpatico. How can she find the strength to make the right choice?

I returned the paper to the cubby, oddly relieved. While I resented Monica's characterization of me as a bad influence— that door swung both ways, thank you—I also realized that her withdrawal had little to do with me personally. I felt certain I was meant to find the letter; it was her way of informing me that she'd embarked on a program of religious cleansing and self-improvement. Giving me up, like chocolate for Lent, was part of it. Sem appeared to be getting under all of our skins.

I got over my hurt and found companionship elsewhere. A few other American girls (and a wayward English classmate I'd discovered) were always good for trips into Newcastle. We branched out from the city center and wandered the narrow medieval streets until we found the university, where we sat on a bench and watched the students hurry to class. We even snuck into a movie once, *Monty Python's Life of Brian,* which we adored.

The third and final term began in May. I landed a three-bed room at last, with ample closets and no Brits. My new roommates were a gentle girl from Cape Town, who was in perpetual chagrin over the twenty-five pounds she'd put on at Sem, and a lanky obsessive from Geneva, whom I would watch in fascination as she ironed her underwear and stockings so they would lie flat on her shelf. She and I developed a companionable "house" friendship, spending evenings together in the small common room, where I would bang out a Scarlatti sonatina on the ancient piano while she cooked us pasta on a hotplate. We shared funny stories about high school and what it was like to be American or Swiss, neither of us much interested in digging deeper.

In June, about a month before we were to break for the year, I was summoned to Mr. Kohn's office. I tapped on the door and heard a raspy, Teutonic "please come in." He was at his desk, slowly going through some papers. A small, elderly, precise man with a snow-white trimmed beard, he sat stiffly in his chair. His eyes seemed to fill the entire frame of his thick spectacles. After leaving Germany, Mr. Kohn had started Gateshead Seminary for the daughters of a small group of fellow refugees. He had devoted his life to nurturing its culture and reputation. That afternoon, he looked concerned.

"Have you been happy here?" he asked.

"Yes," I said, wondering where this was going. "Have you heard something different?"

"Are you still friends with that girl . . ." He struggled for the name. ". . . Monica. I don't think your parents would be happy about it. She's not a good influence on you."

"We're not as close as we used to be," I replied.

He nodded, approvingly, but then got to the point.

"Even so," he continued, "I think you are a girl in Sem, rather than a Sem girl." He paused to let his words sink in. "Perhaps it would be a good idea for you not to return next year."

I was being expelled. And rightly so: I was most certainly not a Sem girl. But having been unexpectedly released, I suddenly wanted nothing more than to stay, panicked by what lay ahead for me. Barnard, I decided, had been a terrible, selfish idea, a vague dream that would only bring sorrow to my family and to me. I owed it to them to do the right thing.

I burst into tears and begged him to reconsider.

"Please, Mr. Kohn, give me another chance. I don't want to leave. I promise I'll do better."

He seemed unconvinced but finally relented. I thanked him profusely and left his office, my eyelids red and puffy. I told no one at Sem about our conversation but called my parents to tell them of my decision. I expected them to be more excited.

"Are you sure?" my mother asked. "Maybe you should think about Israel instead."

"I'm sure. I really like it here," I said, even as my eyes filled with tears yet again.

"Let's talk about it when you get home."

The final day of the term, in late July, coincided with the Tisha B'Av fast, which ended at nightfall. This far north the sun didn't set until close to midnight, and I passed the long day by packing between naps, my head pounding from the lack of caffeine. I'd be home for three weeks and planned to just loll around the house, luxuriating in my own room, my mother's food, my sisters' company, and some catch-up television before I returned to Sem in August to begin my second year.

The next morning I said quick good-byes and left for the Newcastle airport. I checked in for my flight and lined up with the other passengers to board. As I entered the plane something shifted inside me yet again, and as fiercely as I'd wanted to remain in Sem, I knew at once and with great certainty that I would not be returning—not in August, or ever again. That part of my life was over.

12

Stepping Out

The ride from New Haven to Morningside Heights was mostly silent. My father let my mother and me out of the car on Broadway and 120th Street and drove off to find parking while we attempted to get our bearings amid a sweaty welter of young females. Scanning my future classmates, I immediately lasered in on the tawny girls in head-to-toe L.L.Bean, who looked as though they'd just sailed in after a regatta off the Nantucket coast. Prepped by prep school, this was their milieu. Midwestern-looking girls in sensible shorts and haircuts were taking competent possession of the situation, politely negotiating a passage for rolling canvas bins filled with boxes, lamps, rolled-up rugs and posters, laundry baskets, and shopping bags. Some girls had let the tension and the August humidity get the better of them and were arguing with their harried parents. Here and there I noticed someone in a long denim skirt accompanied by a father with a yarmulke, but I saw no beards or *sheitels*. My mother and I, so overwhelmed that we could barely speak, were greeted by a bouncy upperclassman—her T-shirt read WELCOME, BARNARD CLASS OF 1986!—who pointed us to a vague spot past the wrought-iron gates. Inside, we beheld a campus right out of a Hollywood movie: stately brick buildings covered in ivy, majestic columns, and neatly manicured lawns. We approached a check-in table where a packet bearing my name was placed in my hands. By the time my father arrived, triumphantly wheeling a bin into which he had loaded all of my possessions, I'd signed a stack of forms, received my room keys and a Barnard T-shirt, had my ID photo taken, and watched my mother write a hefty check for the kosher meal plan.

The three of us left the campus proper and walked to 116th Street. Passing the Chock full o'Nuts coffee shop on the corner, my parents burst into the famous jingle with its Yiddish-inflected finish: "Better coffee a millionaire's *muh*nee can't buy." I took this as an encouraging sign. The street, which led to Riverside Drive and the park, was lined with dignified turn-of-the-century apartment buildings; once occupied by wealthy families, the flats had been carved up years earlier into suites for Barnard students. We stopped at the last one, where the guard directed us to the fifth floor. By request, I'd been placed in a kosher suite, which consisted of one common room and four bedrooms. Three upperclassmen would arrive the following week and occupy the smaller rooms; the freshman with whom I'd share the larger bedroom had not yet checked in. The suite reeked of paint, fresh slathers of institutional white. In my room, two metal-framed twin beds were pushed against opposite walls, and along the other walls were matching wooden dressers, wardrobes, desks, and chairs. The windows, opened wide to air out the fumes, looked out onto an airshaft and the backsides of four other apartment buildings. My father busied himself unloading the bin.

"Oh, look, it's like Bubby and Zaydie's old apartment, on Eastern Parkway," my mother said, peering into the yard below. She seemed relieved at the similarity to familiar Crown Heights turf. We could hear faint voices coming from somewhere on the other side.

"Yes, it's like Miri's bedroom, at the back," I agreed, eager to reinforce her positive attitude.

She swept the toe of her shoe across a crack in the linoleum. "We'll need to get you a rug. This floor is horrible. And a fan."

My father pointed to the bare door frame. "I have extra mezuzahs. Remind me to give them to you next time."

The kitchen, in the suite's common room, was old but clean, equipped with a small Formica table and vinyl chairs, a fridge, a stove, and white metal cabinets. I had no plans to cook but would need a place to heat water for coffee and store snacks. My mother had bequeathed a few pieces of her old dairy kitchenware to me: plates, cereal bowls, mugs, cutlery, dish towels, and a small lidded pot in case I wanted to boil eggs.

"I wonder if the oven's kosher," my father said. "Or the sink."

"All the girls are kosher, Dad, so probably yes." I sensed trouble brewing.

"But you don't know who lived here last year," he sensibly replied. "Make sure someone *kashers* the stove at least. It's electric, so that's easy. Just turn the burners on high until the coils get red hot, then leave them on for ten minutes. Same with the oven. The sink's a problem. It's ceramic." Unlike metal, ceramic materials cannot be *kashered*. He shot my mother a worried look.

"You'll have to buy a sink rack," my mother said. "Or better yet, a basin, so nothing touches the sides." I assured them I would and started moving toward the door, before they could think of anything else that needed to be religiously upgraded.

Our last stop was on the other side of Broadway, at Columbia's Earl Hall, where the Columbia/Barnard Hillel was located. My mother had called to make an appointment, and a secretary showed us into Rabbi Elias's office. A man who looked to be in his mid-thirties smiled warmly and came around from behind his desk to greet us. He had a pleasant face, with a trimmed strawberry blond beard and a colorful crocheted yarmulke—not too large and not too small, guaranteed to offend no one.

"Shalom," he said. "Please sit down."

We made our introductions. When I mentioned Gateshead, Rabbi Elias's brow twitched slightly. I could see he was trying to figure us out. Barnard probably didn't get many Sem girls.

"Well, obviously Barnard is nothing like Gateshead," he said cautiously, "but I think you'll find that there's a very rich *frum* life here. We have a daily minyan, Shabbos and Yom Tov meals, classes, and so on. Simchas Torah is particularly festive. We get students from all the Ivies."

At the mention of these social gatherings, I envisioned myself hugging the wall in a room full of brilliant and proudly Orthodox men and women from the finest universities in the country. What on earth would I say to these people? At least Shabbos and holiday meals were off the table, so to speak, as I'd promised to come home every Friday.

"What kind of classes?" I asked. Those I could probably handle.

"Oh, quite a few," he replied, ticking off an impressive list of classes in Talmud, Bible, Jewish philosophy, and Jewish law. "Of course, Columbia offers many other courses through its Jewish studies program."

"No *Chassidus*?" my father joked. At the time, Columbia had no Chabad House. Rabbi Elias laughed politely. He ran a tight ship here, brooking no competition from Messianic Lubavitchers.

We chatted for a few more minutes and then my parents rose to leave.

"Well, thank you," my mother said. "This has all been very

helpful. I feel much more reassured." I knew her too well to believe her.

"Not at all," he said. "Between Barnard and Columbia, you'll find a very welcoming community. I look forward to seeing you here often, Chaya."

"Me, too," I said. If I didn't mean it at that very moment, perhaps it would eventually be true.

I walked my parents to their car. As they pulled away and headed back to New Haven, to my sisters and our home, I eased myself back into the stream of pedestrians, suddenly lost and wondering what I'd gotten myself into.

The next day, the freshman class convened in Barnard Hall for orientation. The dean of admissions welcomed us, and I got goose bumps as she ticked off a list of artists, writers, and scientists who had once sat in this very hall: Zora Neale Hurston, Margaret Mead, Laurie Anderson, Patricia Highsmith, Erica Jong. She then got down to the nuts and bolts of student life. After a stern warning not to take the wrong Harlem-bound subway back to campus, she read aloud a passage from a handbook on student conduct: "Students shall respect a ten p.m. weeknight dorm curfew. No men shall be allowed in your rooms. Slacks may not be worn to class." As gasps rippled across the auditorium, I felt a small surge of hope. Perhaps I would fit in after all. Then she let us in on the joke: this was the handbook from 1960.

The woman on my left turned to me, laughing.

"Whew! I actually believed her for a minute." She stuck out her hand. "I'm Ariadne, by the way, and this is Heidi." The woman next to her waved. After the assembly, I tagged along with them to the reception. And thus we became a threesome, going to the movies and sharing pitchers of beer at the West End, a popular student hangout on Broadway. What bound us together was a severe case of impostor syndrome. Ariadne, a WASP from Atlanta, was fulfilling her mother's dream that she attend her alma mater, but she worried that her campus experience would never live up to the stories of sit-ins and antiwar protests she'd grown up on. Heidi, from Long Island, had been the only student in her senior class to get into an Ivy and hoped her rough edges didn't show. As for me, I was entering a civilization whose ways were completely unknown to me, but I was no keen-eyed Margaret Mead, notebook at the ready. The tribal fortress in which I'd been reared had kept me safe but utterly unprepared for the world beyond it. I had no idea how to *be* around people who were not Orthodox Jews; my inner censor was too exacting to allow me simply to say what I was thinking or to jump into new social situations. I was terrified that I would unintentionally commit some sort of gaffe or make an awkward comment. Ever the greenhorn, I wanted not just to belong but to have *always* belonged.

While I was deeply grateful for Heidi and Ariadne's company, our friendship didn't go especially deep. They were both science types and I was more humanities, and, having grown up with no religious identity, they couldn't empathize with my social angst. I'd hoped to find a kindred spirit in my Modern Orthodox roommate, but from the start we just didn't hit it off. She had just come off a life-changing year in a seminary in Israel and still pined for Jerusalem and the friends she'd left behind. When she asked me where I'd gone for seminary, I actually had to think for a minute, so thoroughly had I buried the memory of Gateshead. She didn't appear to think much of the place, and when she found out I'd been raised Chabad, she looked at me as though I'd just told her I was Sikh. We rarely spoke.

I spent my first semester veering between giddiness and panic. I was never happier than when listening to a professor dissect a poem, or curled up in a library armchair with my assigned reading, highlighting passages with neon-yellow streaks. I'd chosen my courses smorgasbord-style: Anthropology, which Ariadne was also taking; Calculus 1 to satisfy my father's desire that I learn something he considered worthwhile; and Astronomy, said to be an easy way to fulfill the science requirement. Literature was my one sure destination, and I began with a class on the nineteenth-century novel, which I chose more because of Professor Maire Janus's reputation for brilliance than for an interest in the literature of that particular era. Blond, tanned, and French, she turned a Nietzschean-Freudian lens onto everything we read. "Eros!" she would growl, scrawling the word on the chalkboard. "Thanatos!" "Dionysius!" "Apollo!" Although most of what she said was beyond me, she gave me an A on my final paper, a "newly discovered" chapter that I'd written for *Alice in Wonderland.*

But even as I threw myself into academics, I shied away from building a social life. Overcome by self-consciousness, I was too timid to speak in class or attend campus events on my own. Fortunately, I found a sympathetic soul in one of my other suitemates. Nina was a fellow English major, and she was sharp, quirky, and wickedly hilarious, with a cackle that turned heads. We both went home for every Shabbos—she to Queens—but weekday evenings we sat on the bed in her tiny room or monopolized the kitchen table, screaming with laughter over nothing. I clung to her friendship; it was a lifeline, even if it would last for only a year.

Like most upperclassmen, Nina chose not to patronize the meal plan, so I ate alone in the kosher dining hall, a room off the main cafeteria that serviced both Barnard and Columbia students. The experience was an eye-opening failure. If the wretchedness of the food—globs of some indefinable protein substance served in aluminum foil pans and eaten off Styrofoam—was barely survivable, the cliquishness of the Modern Orthodox clientele was not. This was the league I'd always aspired to: handsome, clean-shaven men who wore jeans and small, colorful crocheted yarmulkes and were headed toward some high-octane profession; and attractive, smart, career-oriented women who looked effortlessly chic in designer jeans and the Nimrod sandals they'd purchased during their year in Israel. These people dated one another, sampled the allurements of the gentile world, and seemed confident of their Modern Orthodox place in it. Here they were at last, in the same room with me three times a day, my chosen community waiting to embrace me—only they weren't interested and I was too frightened to reach out. Searching for a seat amid animated clusters of friends—almost no one sat alone—I would slip into a chair at the end of a table. From time to time people would turn my way to see if they knew me but would turn back just as quickly when they realized that they didn't. Feigning nonchalance, I would pull a book out of my bag, though my brain was too scrambled to concentrate. I felt simultaneously ridiculous and invisible, as though I'd forgotten to wear clothes and no one noticed.

The dining hall experience blasted away the childhood myths that I'd been fed about what it meant to be Jewish. I'd been taught that religious observance occurred on a kind of sliding scale, with Hasidim and Gateshead types at the pinnacle, and completely assimilated, unobservant Jewish unfortunates at the nadir. In between, in descending level of observance, were Modern Orthodox, Conservative, and Reform Jews. With each step down the ladder, more commandments were discarded as these lesser types opted for taking the easy way out when confronted with the temptations of the outside world. I'd swallowed the model whole, assuming that the lower orders recognized themselves as such and felt appropriately humbled. The possibility that Jews who observed differently than we did might not see it that way—that they embraced, were proud of, and had their own institutional validation for their patterns of observance—had never occurred to me.

As I moved away from Hasidic life, I expected simply to land on a lower rung of Jewish observance. Modern Orthodoxy, just one step down, had always seemed like a comfortable place to stop. After some initial hand-wringing, it would ultimately be acceptable to my parents, and they would be able to survive the gossip about me in Crown Heights; it was nothing compared to the scandal that my complete abandonment of observant Judaism would cause. But I had not counted on being regarded as an outsider by the Modern Orthodox crew in the dining hall. I didn't look like them, I hadn't gone to school or summer camp or Israel with them, and I hadn't come from their neighborhoods. Even after years of close friendships with Modern Orthodox kids in New Haven, I had no idea how to fit in with these people. All I knew was how to be a Lubavitcher, and a bad one at that. I hadn't anticipated the challenge of finding like-minded spirits. Socially inept misfit seeks same. Religious confusion a plus.

I gave up about halfway through first semester and began carrying my kosher meals into the main cafeteria to eat with Heidi and Ariadne. We would eye each other's plates, they warily, me enviously. The experience brought back childhood memories of airline meals on trips to Florida, the disappointment of breaking open the kosher-sealed double wrappings to discover drippy mystery meat, greasy margarine pats, a serviceable roll, and dry marble cake and half-frozen orange segments for dessert. It wasn't long before I peeled the "K" sticker off my student ID and stood in line in the main cafeteria with my friends. Breakfast was easy to rationalize; the cereal, yogurt, and bagels were all kosher, anyhow, and I didn't have a problem using the *trayf* utensils. At lunch, I chose carefully from the salad bar, avoiding all meat—I could barely look at the cubes of gelatinous pink ham—but allowing myself the tuna salad, once again convincing myself that it was kosher enough. Supper I took in my suite, usually leftovers from home or Golden's packaged cheese blintzes, a new favorite since I'd discovered they had only 130 calories each. I was crash-dieting, anyway, trying to shed the pounds I'd gained during my Sem year and then some. With my well-thumbed calorie guide tucked into my book bag alongside *The Complete Works of Geoffrey Chaucer* and French 201, I obsessively totted up columns of numbers, determined not to exceed a self-imposed daily allotment of 1,200 calories. Keeping kosher was easy enough when you weren't eating all that much.

For the time being, there was no temptation to do anything that would violate Shabbos observance. Every Friday I raced for Grand Central to catch the latest train to New Haven I could take and still arrive enough in advance of candle-lighting time so as not to incur my father's wrath. Although I would never have admitted it, coming home was a relief, a respite from the weekday loop of social anxiety, self-censuring, and loneliness. At Shabbos dinner, I monopolized the conversation, entertaining my parents and sisters with stories about my professors and campus adventures with Nina. Afterward, sprawled on the living room carpet with my class reading, I'd observe my sisters and the new configuration of power that had formed in my absence. Ricki seemed to be thriving in the role of resident eldest daughter, ruling the roost but with a lighter touch than I'd ever managed. She would go to seminary in Jerusalem the following year, and in the meantime was entertaining herself with complicated art projects and a secret boyfriend. I envied her attractiveness to boys and couldn't help but feel resentful of my role as family trailblazer, the one with no model to follow, who made it easier for all the sisters who came after her.

Glaringly absent from my dinnertime tales was any mention of the Columbia/Barnard Jewish life that Rabbi Elias had laid out for us that first week. No stories about Hillel socials or lessons learned at Bible-portion-of-the-week class. That first year, my parents asked about it constantly.

"But you said you would," my mother would complain when I confessed I'd not gotten around to checking out the Hillel offerings. Each time, I would promise that I'd sign up for a class that very week, knowing that nothing would come of it. My best hope was that they would eventually get the message or at least tire of asking about it. Of my social failure in the kosher dining hall I said nothing—and certainly not that I'd stopped going.

My lack of involvement with the Modern Orthodox crowd came to a head in late spring, during the dorm lotteries for the following September. The kosher students generally applied in blocs of three, to increase their chances of getting their first choice of suitemates. With Nina graduating and my roommate deciding to commute instead of dorm, I assumed that for my sophomore year I'd room with the two remaining upperclassmen from my freshman suite. I was wrong. We'd never really clicked during the school year, and when they invited another friend of theirs to join their group, I was on my own. Hopelessly unconnected, I could find no one who needed a kosher suitemate. I considered my options. Heidi and Ariadne both preferred traditional dorm rooms, with a single shared bathroom and no kitchen. If I joined them, I would have to sign up again for the kosher meal plan, and the idea of communal living brought back traumatic memories of the dorm at Sem. In the end, I took a chance on a single room in a nonkosher suite right above my old kosher suite, crossing my fingers that at the very least I'd find another friend. I also hoped the proximity to my former suitemates would mollify my parents, but they were livid.

"How are you going to eat?" my father said. "What if you want to make breakfast? You can't even wash your dishes in the sink."

"The girls downstairs said I could use their kitchen whenever I want," I lied.

"Was it really that hard to get into a kosher suite?" my mother demanded. "I feel like you're selling us a bill of goods here. What's happening to you?"

"I tried, but there's a limited number of spots!" My voice trembled with indignation but, as my mother guessed, I hadn't exactly beaten the bushes for kosher housing. What stung, however, was the implication that I was carrying out a deliberately mapped strategy to rebel. This was patently untrue. A plan required agency, desire, free will, independence—admirable traits on paper but too frightening for me to own up to or, God forbid, embrace. I talked a good game, but underneath my bravado lurked a constant, achy dread: that I had overreached, snapped my tether, and would end up drifting and alone. Whom could I grab on to if not my family? What I wanted was separateness from them, not an unbridgeable distance. Adopting a more unplanned, impulsive approach to life seemed to be the safest route to staying close to them. Better to pretend that things simply "happened" and that I couldn't be held accountable for them. I convinced myself that my small fabrications and omissions were actually a kindness to my parents, protecting them from a truth they couldn't handle. But even this was false. I did it for myself, creating fictions that I believed would keep me bound to my family even as I propelled myself into a new orbit. There seemed to be no other way to make a grab for freedom while clinging to the comfort of fulfilling my parents' expectations.

In fact, my fear of being banished from the house, as my unobservant great-uncle and great-aunt had been back in Russia, had no basis in reality. My parents were as unwilling to let me go as I was to leave. It was unclear to me whether they believed my version of events, but they never out-and-out accused me of lying and never threatened to cut off my tuition. Perhaps they couldn't envision how far off the path I might travel, or perhaps I was an extremely good liar. They certainly sniffed trouble but most likely didn't know what to do about it. This was new ground for all of us.

When I returned home at the end of freshman year, my goal for the summer was simply to avoid confrontation. It would not be easy. While I was away at Gateshead, my family had moved to a new house around the corner from our old one. It was larger but with fewer bedrooms. With my childhood possessions boxed up in the attic, I bunked with my six-year-old sister Suri and her menagerie of ceramic and plush animals, all of whom had prior claim to the space. I had no plans for the next three months other than a two-week stint in July at the plastics factory, where I'd man the phones while the receptionist was away. My high school friends were gone for the summer, and a desultory job search proved fruitless; I'd hoped to work as a shelf stocker at my old haunt, the Atticus Bookstore, but they weren't hiring.

My time at the switchboard came none too soon. Every morning, I drove to work with my father and planted myself at Lucille's immaculate desk, taking calls from handbag manufacturers, accountants, loan officers, truck drivers, and relatives looking for husbands and fathers. Lucille, who had been with the company for years, embodied the Platonic ideal of receptionists and had fretted over what might happen during her absence. She'd had me come in the week before for training, and while I couldn't hope to master her astonishing recall of names and voices, I quickly got the hang of the technology and could even imitate her breathy regret when I said, "I'm so sorry, Mr. Bachman, can you hold for a minute more?" My grandfather, who never once asked me about college, was impressed.

"Smart girl," he said, stroking my hair. Living up to Zaydie's expectations for me certainly wasn't hard: I knew how to work the phones.

When I returned to Broadway and 116th Street in late August, I turned the key to my bedroom and nearly wept with relief when I cautiously opened the door. A pie-shaped sliver toward the back of the suite, it had just enough space for a narrow twin bed, a dresser, and a small desk and chair. I loved every inch of it; the door locked and it was mine, alone. I unpacked quickly, dressed the bed with my new Indian print spread, and left to hunt down Heidi and Ariadne, whom I'd not spoken to all summer. Returning that evening, I found a chubby young man in the bedroom next to mine. He was standing in front of the mirror cementing his black spiked hair with a stream of Aquanet, his lit cigarette a fuse poised to turn him into a cautionary tale. He caught me watching him and turned around.

"Hi, I'm Anton."

"Chaya. We share a wall," I said, gesturing toward my room.

"Katherine just ran out to buy some food. She'll be back soon."

With the dart I'd thrown the previous spring for my room assignment, I'd managed to hit a bull's-eye. Katherine and I were remarkably simpatico—we were both studious English majors and, perhaps most important, both recovering refugees from girls' parochial schools, Catholic in Katherine's case. Uncomfortable in groups, we masked our awkwardness with disdain for anything that smacked of convention. Katherine, a New York City native, had established a style that was gloriously her own. In contrast to the showy fur coats and glitter that had started sprouting on campus—this was the mid-1980s—she wore a black leather coat à la Johnny Cash, elegant black eyeliner, a slight sneer, and a single dangling feather earring that peeped through her long brown curls. I emulated her look as best I could, adopting her cigarette brand, Export As, and appropriating my father's boxy gray herringbone coat, which he'd purchased when I was still in diapers. When I asked if I could take it, he was horrified at the thought of my wearing it in public.

"I still use it sometimes," he insisted.

"Go ahead, then," I said, handing it to him to try on. We both laughed as he struggled to close it over his generous front. I peeled it off his shoulders, pinned a small Marilyn Monroe button onto the lapel, and wore it on the train back to New York.

I had no punked-out boyfriend, of course. Anton technically dormed at Columbia, but he spent nearly every night in our suite, mashed next to Katherine in her tiny bed. The three of us hung out together most evenings, gabbing in our kitchen as we downed giant bowls of Häagen-Dazs vanilla Swiss almond ice cream, got drunk on cheap red wine, and filled the ashtray to overflowing. Occasionally we ventured outside to take in a film at one of the Upper West Side art house cinemas: *Fanny and Alexander, Seven Samurai, Andrei Rublev.* That Katherine wasn't Jewish made our friendship even more appealing. It was a relief not to have to respond to prying questions about Lubavitchers or argue over whose grandma made better chicken soup. I didn't ask about Jesus and she'd never even heard of the Rebbe. The only flaw in this picture-perfect world was that Katherine was a senior, which meant that next September I'd once again be on my own.

Although I was still keeping Shabbos and eating my version of kosher, midway through my sophomore year I decided I was ready to step, literally, back into pants—something I'd been dreaming of since my bas mitzvah. I began with baggy sweatpants, which I discounted as workout clothes, pajamas really, and which I just happened to wear to class. (In actual fact, they never saw a gym; I was fulfilling my physical education requirement with bowling.) Jeans were the greater hurdle. Unlike quietly consuming a questionable slab of lasagna in a corner of the campus dining hall, wearing jeans would be en plein air, a public act of religious defiance. For Lubavitchers and other *frum* Jews, a woman never just wore pants, she officially "wore pants," which definitively broadcast her position as Modern-Orthodox-verging-on-who-knows-what on the observance spectrum. It made a bold statement in a way that above-the-elbow sleeves or above-the-knee hemlines never did.

A seasoned shopper, I was surprised at how hard it was to find pants that fit. My first stop was the Gap, for Levi's; to my disappointment, they were too straight-legged for my curvy lower half. Next was Macy's, but the skintight Calvin Kleins I tried on were a pipe dream. In the end, I settled for generic trouser-cut jeans with cuffed hems and front pleats from Bolton's, a discount clothing chain. Although the style was a touch matronly, they made my waist look tiny and rounded my rear end spectacularly. I did not expect to love them as much as I did, and not just for comfort or fashion or because they helped me blend into most places. Like Wonder Woman's golden wristlets, my jeans made me feel powerful. Pulling them on, mingling them in the closet with my skirts and dresses, learning to sit and walk differently, even tossing them into the wash—they signified my newfound independence, if to no one other than myself.

But at the same time, I lived in mortal fear of encountering some member of my family while dressed in my inappropriate garb. One afternoon, I unexpectedly spotted my aunt Nechama and her daughter strolling toward me on Broadway. Busy talking to each other, they didn't notice me, but I could feel a rush of adrenaline as my heart began to race and my face turned bright red. It was a classic example of fight or flight—and I fled, ducking into a Korean deli until it seemed safe to leave. I wondered if there would ever come a time when I could feel just like any other person walking down a street.

I sometimes thought about my ease in crossing over into sin. Perhaps I was repressing my true feelings—I'd been reading a lot of Freud—but it didn't feel that way. The tit-for-tat concept of divine retribution had never made sense to me: how could God possibly care that I turned on the hot water faucet on Shabbos? Or even ate bacon, should it come to that? Surely He operated on a scale that was way beyond my insignificant goings-on. Neither could I square the idea that religious belief was absolute. Reform Jews or Christians could be just as devout within their belief systems as Orthodox Jews were within theirs. Jews who drove to shul on Shabbos would feel pious if they were Reform but ashamed if they were Orthodox. Faith, and so-called spirituality, from which I derived neither strength nor solace, seemed to come down to nothing more than personal choice. My mother's accusation in high school, that I thought like a "damned humanist," reverberated in my head as I proceeded to jack-hammer the foundations of my religious observance, turning into rubble two decades of yeshiva education and generations of customs and traditions for which my ancestors were willing to give their lives. I suppose I was a humanist. I just didn't find anything damning about it.

My parents' feelings were much less easily dismissed. I felt plenty of angst where they were concerned: remorse for the condescending sympathy I was sure would be heaped upon them in the Lubavitcher community because of me, shame over their almost certain disappointment in my choices, worry that I would take my sisters down with me, fear that my family would one day decide to cut me loose, and fury that I had to fight so hard to live what other people considered a simple, ordinary life. If I pleaded no contest with God, in the court of filial duty I was amassing a long rap sheet of crimes and misdemeanors.

13

On My Way

I did one more pocket check for my wallet and keys and hurried to the elevator, where Ellen, my junior-year suitemate, was holding the door for me.

"Sorry to be late," I said. "Anal retentive."

"Tell me about it! But we better get moving before tickets sell out. It's Friday night." Friday night. By now it barely registered on my consciousness. We were on our way to see *The Lady from Shanghai*, part of a Rita Hayworth film festival, after a quick dinner in our suite. Ellen had half-jokingly referred to the roast chicken with vegetables as our Shabbos dinner, but I could tell that the idea touched a sentimental nerve within her, a link to her mother's sepia-toned stories about growing up in Brooklyn. Having herself grown up as a completely assimilated Jew—her family celebrated Christmas—Ellen had developed an irritating fascination with my Orthodox roots. Although we got on well, I often felt flattened around her, transmuted from friend to *frum* poster girl, the way Alvy Singer felt at Annie Hall's parents' dinner table, as he mentally sprouted a black hat, beard, and *peyos*. I allowed that this just might be me being overly sensitive. I had no interest in being exotic. I wanted no part of Friday night Shabbos dinner, but at the same time I was also hyper-defensive about outsiders' half jokes about the world in which I'd grown up. I couldn't tell if they were being wistful or mocking; either option stung.

I'd abandoned Shabbos in stages, starting late in my sophomore year by turning the lights on and off in my dorm room—after all, it doesn't say anywhere in the Bible that you can't. Smoking came next, a sin I rationalized because it was permitted on Jewish holidays. By junior year, I was accepting Friday night invitations from Ariadne to meet at the West End for a beer, but asking her to pay for me. I still felt uncomfortable handling money, although for some reason I had no qualms about answering the phone when she called or taking the elevator downstairs. At first, my transgressions would bring up a whisper of sadness, a vague sense of something lost. I waited for the onrush of guilt, but it never came. Mostly my new life felt strange, like putting on a pair of three-inch heels after wearing flats for a long time. Everything looked just a little different on "Saturday," as I was beginning to think of it, whether it was my fellow passengers on the subway or the stores that I shopped in, wallet in hand. Eventually, over the course of my junior year, even the oddness disappeared, leaving a mere residue of awareness, a puff of memory of what Shabbos used to be. This, I realized, was why the rabbis had put "fences" around the Shabbos prohibitions: don't pick up a pencil lest you accidentally begin to write with it, don't even touch money or you might be tempted to spend it. They knew how easy it was to cross over.

As my weekends became more social, I went back to New Haven less frequently. I invented a vibrant *frum* social life for my parents' benefit, conjuring invitations to Friday night dinner or Shabbos lunch from equally imaginary friends; when I called my parents on Sunday, my recounting included detailed rundowns of what was served at the meals. The lies slipped off my tongue, but I felt sick each time and needed hours to recover. I'd grown adept at other falsifications as well. Friday night movies moved to Thursday, dinner at a local café was relocated to the kosher Famous Dairy Restaurant on Seventy-Second Street. But even as I continued to thrust and parry in conversations with my parents, I assumed they knew what I was up to. How could they not? My stories were starting to get knotted up—the long hesitation as I tried frantically to recall the name of the rabbi of the shul where I told them I *davened,* not being in my suite for my parents' usual phone call right before Shabbos candle lighting, "forgetting" what I'd ordered at dinner with friends at Moshe Peking the night before. I could tell by their quiet, monosyllabic responses that my parents didn't believe me, but to my vast relief they never called me on it.

This was not how my liberation was meant to go. I wanted my parents to know about what was happening, to sit them down for "the talk." In my fantasies, I would simply rip off the Band-Aid and tell them that I wore pants, that I no longer kept kosher or observed Shabbos, and that I would one day have an adult life that looked different from theirs. I would apologize for hurting them and compromising their standing in the Lubavitcher community. I would also remind them how much I loved and needed them. It was going to be honest and mature, not without tears, of course, but culminating in embraces, acceptance, and encouragement all around—like something out of *The Waltons,* I imagined. Or if I really stepped into another dimension of time and space, my parents would start the discussion for me. "Darling," they would say, "we know you've been struggling to tell us that you're not *frum* anymore. Well, we already know and that's just fine. Nothing matters to us more than your happiness."

We never even came close. Neither my parents nor I had the language or, I suppose, the courage for something this immense. So we fought instead. They were angry and confused, and felt that I had not lived up to my part of the bargain that we'd made when they let me attend Barnard.

Most of the arguments with my father were over silly little things; all that repressed tension needed to go someplace. The fights with my mother were more fraught. One Shabbos afternoon, my father returned from shul with two young men, rabbinical students from the local yeshiva. This was not unusual. Over the years we'd hosted a stream of nineteen- and twenty-year-olds who dormed at the yeshiva and would join us for meals and a brief immersion in family life. When I was a teenager, they modestly avoided addressing or even looking at me; I'd be prospective bride material in a few years. Now that I was twenty-two and virtually aged out as a marriage prospect, I wondered whether I would seem safer to converse with, as my mother and little sisters were. These two guests were particularly shy, however, nodding a slight thanks when I cleared their fish plates but otherwise ignoring me and even my mother. They engaged solely with my father, who tried to bring them out by asking them what they thought of the talk delivered in shul that day, which was about the relationship of science to Torah. It was a subject on which the Rebbe had often written—I had read some of his translated essays—and it had clearly touched a nerve with one of the boys.

"Science is based on theories and experiments," he said excitedly, "but the Torah is absolute fact, given by Hashem to Moshe on Mount Sinai. So how can we say that the world *isn't* six thousand years old? Everything else is speculation."

My father nodded.

"It's interesting," the young man continued. "The Zohar predicted that in the Jewish year 5600, which was 1840, there would be a big discovery. This is right around the time that Hasidic teachings were spread around the world. So, really, *Chassidus* is the wisdom that brings together science and Torah."

"Nostradamus said the world would end in the year 2000," I interjected. I knew I was being provocative, but I was annoyed by the conversation and tired of being frozen out.

"Who?" my father asked.

"Nostradamus. He was a French astrologer from the sixteenth century who predicted all kinds of weird stuff that came true." My father hadn't heard of him, but then he wasn't as devoted a reader of *Ripley's Believe It or Not* as I was.

"That's ridiculous," he said. "Why would people still believe him?"

"Who knows? But he was a big deal in his day." I ran to get the *Encyclopaedia Britannica*. Hauling the relevant volume to the table, I pointed triumphantly to the entry. My father gave it a cursory read and grinned at me. He seemed to enjoy my one-upping him, and it was nice that someone at the table had finally acknowledged my existence. I went into the kitchen to help my mother bring out the next course and found her angrily slicing a roast. She put down the knife when I approached.

"Why are you showing off?" she hissed, so mad that she could barely get the words out.

"What are you talking about?" I hissed back. We were out of view but the kitchen door was open.

"You're making the boys uncomfortable."

I stared at her, her words stabbing me in the chest. Sure, I'd been a little confrontational, but it was mostly directed at my father and he seemed not to mind it.

"That's not true!" was all I could get out. Why was she protecting them instead of looking out for me?

"Oh, please!" she replied, glaring at me as she slammed a platter full of sliced meat on the counter. "You know they don't know about those types of things. It's bad enough that you're creating all this conflict at home. I don't need you showing off in front of company. Here." She angrily pointed at the meat.

"It's not true," I repeated, although I had to admit to myself that it was, at least partially, true. I snatched the heaping plate from the counter and carried it into the dining room, hot with shame and outrage.

My sisters, involuntary witnesses to these mealtime explosions, each reacted differently. All the hostility went largely over the head of eight-year-old Suri. Bayla, now ten, was more sensitive to these disruptions, and I could see that she was frightened by the rage and upset I'd brought into the house; the bad feelings would linger long after I returned to school on Sunday. Ella watched with a more vested interest: a freshman in high school, she was collecting fuel for future expressions of her own discontent.

More often than not, Ricki was absent. After her seminary year in Israel, she'd convinced my parents to let her attend Parsons School of Design in Manhattan to pursue a degree in illustration. My mother, herself a skilled painter, was sympathetic to Ricki's creative urges, if apprehensive about letting her go to art school.

But Ricki had worn them down and sworn that she would not follow in my troublesome footsteps. Instead of dorming, she was now sharing an apartment on the Upper West Side with three other Orthodox girls. This gave her a built-in alibi for Shabbos.

But in actual fact, she and I were aiding and abetting each other in our mutual flight from religion. When Ricki moved to New York that fall, it took no more than a few weeks for each of us to confess that we'd started wearing pants. That she'd begun to do so on her own absolved me of at least some responsibility, and it was a relief for both of us to have someone who fully understood the magnitude of what we were leaving behind. But the first time Ricki publicly violated Shabbos was with me, when we went into a deli to buy cigarettes (for me) and some bagels for a picnic in Riverside Park. Before long we were eating out together at nonkosher cafés. We were surprised by how natural it felt.

I entered senior year finally experiencing the college life I'd dreamed of as a teenager in New Haven. I had cobbled together a small group of good friends. I made myself a fixture in the English Department, and although I was still reluctant to speak up in class, the lectures and reading thrilled me as much as ever; the sheer pleasure of connecting A to B to C in a text sometimes made me laugh out loud. I became obsessed with medieval lit (and delighted in reciting the beginning stanzas of *The Canterbury Tales* in flawless Middle English) and my professors were pushing me toward graduate school. I began to attract the attention of men, some of whom sent me shy notes. I also began to acquaint myself with Manhattan's commercial and cultural glories: forays to Canal Jeans in SoHo, double features at the Thalia, art exhibits at the Met and MoMA, hours at the Strand perusing musty shelves of used books.

At the same time, I had more or less settled into the double life that would be the pattern for much of my twenties and thirties; I felt like I was at the center of a Venn diagram, with cherished but distinct spheres that overlapped to varying degrees and in ever-changing ways but that could never completely coincide. My parents got highly edited versions of my New York life: the museums and shopping excursions, of course, and sometimes the drinking—judiciously censored, it kept things sounding real. I gabbed away to my mother about my classes, passing along the art history texts and the readings for my class in feminist literary theory, which I thought she would find interesting. I brought home a few friends whom I knew would pass muster: Ellen, lover of all things Brooklyn, although her interactions with my family needed my constant supervision, and Amy, my senior-year suitemate, a knowledgeable Conservative Jew from Toronto who could be counted on not to let the wrong pieces of information slip. Once, on a lark, I even took my very Teutonic-looking friend Laurel to Crown Heights, to visit Bubby Gurewitz. She was delighted to see us, feeding us coffee and cake, and peppering us in Yiddish with questions. Laurel gamely responded in German, a distinction my mostly deaf grandmother seemed not to catch.

"*Deinen elter'n, zayn'n zay doh?*" Bubby asked.

"*Vie, bitte?*" Laurel's German wasn't helping here.

"*Die elter'n. . . .*"

I tried to translate. "She's asking about your grandparents—either where they live or whether they're alive. I'm not sure."

"Ja," Laurel cheerfully replied. "Tenafly, New Jersey."

Aside from visits to my grandparents, I'd been consciously putting some distance between myself and my extended family since I'd moved to New York. I still went to my cousins' weddings in Crown Heights; blood counted for something, and even those brief touch points reminded me that I still felt attached to my aunts, uncles, and cousins. But while I was genuinely glad to see everyone for a few hours, we had less and less to talk about. After politely nodding at the inevitable "God willing you'll be next," exclaiming over each other's dresses, and promising to meet for lunch in Manhattan, we ran out of things to say. Or, rather, I did. Chattering about my classes and other activities would naturally lead to questions about what I did for Shabbos, or whether I'd met the newly arrived Chabad guy who was setting up a Chabad House not far from Columbia. It was hard enough managing these issues with my parents; I had little stomach for spreading my lies outward.

I was certainly pleased that men were noticing me; I just wasn't sure what I was going to do about it. I met Jeff at a dinner party hosted by my former suitemate Katherine, who had taken a job at a nonprofit after graduation. We flirted for a while, but I was still surprised to hear his voice on the phone a few days later. No boy had ever actually hunted down my phone number and called me for a date. I liked him—he had that wry midwestern sense of humor I was partial to, and he was even Jewish. It was fun to be part of a couple as we looked at the dioramas at the Museum of Natural History. Back in my dorm room we kissed and fooled around a bit, but that was as far as I could go. Even after a few more dates I wasn't ready to cross the line into deeper intimacy, despite years of breathlessly imagining what it would be like. Underneath the jeans and the vintage blouses, the funky jewelry and the cigarettes, cowered a frightened Hasidic girl who just wanted to be left alone. Sex, and the closeness that came with it, would expose me both physically and emotionally in ways that I was not yet able to share, with anyone. I cooled toward Jeff, and he finally got the message and stopped calling.

By now, however, the Lubavitcher matchmaking engine was in full throttle on my behalf, and I could no more halt it than I could a real locomotive. It was a given that the time had come for me to marry, and when I returned from Gateshead, my parents began fielding a flow of calls from relatives and Crown Heights connections, who eagerly passed on information about noteworthy families with single sons. Even with the blot of college on my résumé, my Deitsch and Gurewitz pedigree still made me a good Lubavitcher catch. Many of these early candidates were top scholars at their yeshivas, praised by their rabbis. They were unquestionably men of fine character, often with aspirations of running their own campus Chabad Houses. To these prospects, my parents gave a polite but firm refusal: the life of a rebbetzin was not what they had in mind for their daughters. The son-in-law they envisioned would be in business or a profession, perhaps even college-educated, worldly but from a good family. When someone who fit the profile was recommended, one of my parents would call and float the idea of my meeting him. My default answer was always no. I wasn't ready, I'd argue. Or I'd say that he sounded too *frum,* that I'd heard he was unattractive, or that he had been recommended by someone whose opinion I didn't trust. My rejections, delivered in accusatory tones and sometimes in tears, mystified my parents. They couldn't understand why I wasn't interested in dating. They made it clear that there would be no pressure on me to decide immediately, or to do anything against my will, but they found my attitude puzzling nonetheless.

"What's the harm in one date?" my father asked. "You don't like him, you don't have to see him again."

"You act like we're trying to sell you to the highest bidder," my mother said indignantly. "We just want you to be happy."

All true, I knew, but with me still unwilling to come clean about what I wanted for my life, we were having two different conversations.

Finally, I ran out of excuses. Someone suggested a Lubavitcher boy from Los Angeles, a more "modern" type, a student at Yeshiva University majoring in accounting. His sister and I had been camp bunkmates years earlier. I agreed to meet him. He called a few days later and we set up a date for that Saturday night. When I told my mother that he seemed nice on the phone, she was ecstatic.

Kobi and I had planned to see a movie, and I spent Saturday afternoon assembling my outfit. I figured he might as well know where I stood from the get-go, so I aimed for a look that was a fusion of demure, sexy, edgy, and inscrutable, part beatnik and part punk: black turtleneck, above-the-knee denim skirt, dangly skull earrings, and black leather lace-up boots. As eight o'clock neared I started to get nervous, and almost in spite of myself I began to wonder, *Could I possibly fall in love with this guy?*

Kobi arrived at eight on the dot. He was undeniably handsome— California tanned, nicely built, and of medium height. He was acceptably dressed in jeans, a crew-neck sweater, and a crocheted yarmulke. His beard, alas, was untrimmed, but everything else looked good. And he *was* nice, friendly like his sister, not afraid to look me in the eye. Our conversation was easy, and we kept it confined to safe topics—our classes, people we both knew, things we liked about New York, movies, rock music. Unshared, of course, was the fact that I was not Modern Orthodox, but completely off the religious charts and with no interest in returning—not even, I was beginning to realize, for someone who met all of my other requirements. I knew that without this common ground, all other points of compatibility were immaterial. Kobi and I went back to my room after the movie for cookies and beer, and to listen to my mix tapes. With so much of my life off-limits, by one a.m. we'd run out of things to talk about. I agreed to another date for the following week—I had no excuse for turning him down—and he left. My mother called me early the next morning for details.

"I had fun," I admitted. "He's very nice. He looks like his sister Leora."

"He does? She's very attractive. Where did you go?" I could almost see her eyes sparkling, her inner romantic unleashed.

"The new Woody Allen movie. It was really good."

"Do you think you'll see him again?"

"Yes, next Saturday night."

She tried to play it cool, but I could tell that underneath she was thrilled.

"I'm glad," she said simply, and with impressive restraint. "You'll see how it goes."

We had our second date at a plush pool hall in Chelsea, but it was awkward from the start. We had already tapped the most superficial stuff—first dates were easy, I realized—but now neither of us had much to say. I wasn't really interested in getting to know him better, and I certainly didn't want to share any more of my life story with him. We spent most of the night studying the arrangement of the balls on the pool table, as though waiting for them to reveal the mysteries of the ages. In the tight space, Kobi's arm brushed against mine a few times, and I felt a warm tingle of attraction. But there was no point in going any further with this. I would have to dash my mother's hopes. If Kobi and I had clicked, he would want marriage to follow immediately, but this was something I was not yet ready for. I was determined to get my bachelorette pad. I envisioned a sunny apartment in SoHo, Tribeca, or Greenwich Village, on one of those narrow old cobblestone streets where I'd always lose my way. I'd even decorated it in my head: overstuffed shabby-chic sofa, distressed wood table and chairs, and lots of salmon-colored accents. Marriage could wait. I had plenty of time, even if my parents didn't think so.

A few months later, on a warm morning in May, my parents and I once again made our way through the crowds milling at the Barnard gates. It was their first time back on campus grounds since they'd moved me in four years earlier. Following the graduation ceremony, I planned to return with them to New Haven for a bit, but I had a busy summer ahead of me. Some friends and I had sublet a professor's apartment on Riverside Drive, and I'd lined up an interview for a publishing job at Penguin Books. And I planned to apply to graduate school for the following year. In late June, Amy and I were going to Mexico City for a week with two male friends of hers. Marcus, the cute one, had been flirting with me since we'd met several weeks earlier. I'd given my parents an edited description of the trip; there was no way I could disappear for a week without stirring panic. They agreed that I deserved a vacation. Of Marcus, they knew nothing. This was just how it was going to be.

I deftly led my mother, father, and Ricki through the throngs until we arrived at the seats I'd saved on the far side of the lawn, strategically situated in the cool shadow of the science building. It was getting hot and we still had the ceremony on the Columbia campus to attend that afternoon. My parents looked happy, if a little lost. On the way in, they noticed the kosher box lunches stacked on a table. Very thoughtful, my father remarked. I hugged them and left to line up with my class. A lump formed in my throat with the first strains of the processional music—a flute solo of a classical piece I didn't recognize. I entered my designated row and settled down for the speeches. Speaker after speaker reminded us that graduation was a commencement, not an ending, the first step toward bigger things. Nothing to disagree with there.

At last, the dean of students called my name (during rehearsal, I saw her make a small note about the guttural Hebrew "ch"), and I walked onstage to accept my degree and shake hands with Ellen Futter, Barnard's president. The teenager from Beth Chana-Hannah Academy who had been terrified that she would flunk out of an Ivy League school hadn't done too badly: magna cum laude, dean's list, honors in English, and a special award for medieval studies. As I flipped the tassel from the right side of my mortarboard to the left, I was struck by the significance, the permanence, of what I'd just accomplished. Today was a beginning, to be sure, but there was also a blissful, irrefutable finality to it. This was something I had done, and it would be mine forever.

But it wasn't just mine, of course. Four years earlier, I'd stepped through an unknown door, dragging my reluctant parents and my sisters behind me. Because of me, nothing would ever be the same for any of us. "Children stretch you," my mother would later remark wistfully—a profound understatement given the unexpected turn her eldest child had taken and the grief my parents had gotten from friends and relatives over their decision to let me go to Barnard. There would be more to come, we knew. And yet on that extraordinary morning, as I ran back toward their seats, clutching the hem of my gown to keep from tripping, they beamed as though we'd all won the lottery and waved at me to come faster.

Afterword

Secrets, and sometimes even lies, can often be a kindness. Not everyone needs to know everything about everybody. The Torah specifically prohibits one type of untruth, bearing false witness, but halachah, Jewish law, parses some white lies, under specific circumstances, with a little more flexibility. What we choose to reveal about ourselves is for us to decide. But secrecy can also force us to silence some essential part of ourselves; dissembling, you do not appear as you truly are.

Like many children of immigrants, I grew up carrying old baggage in a new world. My history encompasses wars and gulags, but also resilience, loyalty, and faith. One of the more durable lessons of that history has been to wall off your enemies and keep family close. But what happens when *you're* the stranger in the midst of your world? Then you float uncomfortably, unable (or unwilling) to share with your family the person you have become in the world even as you set your stakes down on it. I did that for a very long time.

My adult relationship with my parents grew *around* my secrecy, like new skin covering an old wound. When I was with them, I pretended that the chunks of my existence that I had to keep from them simply didn't exist, and I put a premium on the parts of my life that I was able to share with them. That wasn't ideal, but kindness and good intentions pulled us through. At the same time, I've built a robust life for myself: a career in finance, moves from New York to Los Angeles and back to New York, occasional boyfriends. My bachelorette pad, on a crooked street in Manhattan's West Village, is a "little jewel" in real estate parlance: a cozy one-bedroom similar in spirit, if not in actual décor, to the apartment I envisioned as a teenager, many years ago. When I'm not working, I cook for friends, travel abroad and across the country, and go out for probably too many fancy cocktails. My sisters have married and had children, and I am one of a smother of aunts, with nieces and nephews to indulge.

Completing this book at long last forced me to make an honest woman of myself. My parents had known I was writing a memoir, but I'd been skittish about letting them see any part of the manuscript, afraid that anticipating a negative reaction would make me censor myself even before I got the words down. Well before this book was published, however, my editor strongly advised me to show it to them. "There's a lot of *stuff* in there," she said. So I screwed up my courage, told my parents "it's time," and went to New Haven for Shabbos with two copies of the manuscript in my bag. I sat my parents down in the living room, the story of my life resting on my lap. I'd been practicing this conversation all week.

"Before I give you these, it seems only right that we talk about the fact that I'm no longer *frum* and haven't been so for a long time." I felt faint. It was the first time I'd actually said these words to them. "You shouldn't have to learn about it from a book."

My mother cocked an eyebrow. "You think we didn't know? That's why I don't call you at home on Friday before Shabbos. I don't want to make you lie to me."

"You chose a different life," my father said. "Of course we knew about it."

I nodded, but I wasn't quite finished. "I also want to say that I'm not going to lie to you anymore. It's takes too much out of me and I think it's been bad for our relationship. I will spare you the details of what I eat, but when I travel on Shabbos, I'm not changing the day to Sunday when I tell you about it."

They nodded, silently, not looking terribly enthused.

"And I need your help," I continued. "Even though I'm being straight with you now, it will be difficult for me not to slip back into my old habits. I've fudged the truth with you for so long, it's hard to stop. So I'm asking you to make it easier for me by remembering that I will sometimes do that. Please just understand and don't ask the wrong questions."

"Of course," my mother said. "I'll try my best."

I handed her the manuscript and she smiled at me, a little nervously.

I turned to my father, who swiftly took a pass on reading his copy. It was not his thing; I understood.

"Just sell a bunch of copies," he said. I smiled at his effort to be supportive. And, like that, it was done.

Acknowledgments

This book took its sweet time coming into the world, with a lot of people nudging it—and me—forward. A huge thanks to Charles Salzberg and his Monday night New York Writers Workshop, whose thoughtful feedback and encouragement got me over the hump and helped to give shape to the story. I'm especially grateful to the Sallies Koslow and Hoskins and to Vivian Conan, my cheerleaders and doulas throughout the gestation of this book. I could not have finished it without you. My thanks and love to my dear friends Michele Rubin and Sheryl Freedland.

Deep, deep gratitude to my agent, Jane Dystel, for her industry acumen, wise counsel, and for delivering me into the magical hands of Altie Karper, my editor at Schocken. She immediately "got" this story and made it so much better than I would have thought possible. Many thanks as well to my publicist, Jordan Rodman, for her hard work and enthusiasm.

And, finally, there will never be enough thank-yous for my amazing family—Mom, Dad, and the other four heads of the Deitsch Sister-Monster—who not only allowed me to drag them along on this difficult journey but also, together with my wonderful brothers-in-law and nieces and nephews, supported me every step of the way. You're the coolest people I know.